WHERE
ANGELS
WALK

# WHERE ANGELS WALK

## True Stories of Heavenly Visitors

## JOAN WESTER ANDERSON

Barton & Brett, Publishers, Inc.
Sea Cliff, New York

Grateful acknowledgment is made to the following for permission to reprint previously published material:

Chosen Books (Old Tappan, NJ, 1986): Excerpt from *Angels Watching Over Me* by Betty Malz. Copyright © 1986 by Fleming H. Revell Co. Reprinted by permission.

*Guideposts* magazine: "The Day We Saw the Angels" by Dr. S. Ralph Harlow. Copyright © 1970 Guideposts Associates, Inc., Carmel, NY. Reprinted by permission.

All Scripture quotations are taken from the HOLY BIBLE, NEW INTERNATIONAL VERSION, Copyright © 1973, 1978, 1984 by International Bible Society. Used by permission of Zondervan Publishing House.

ISBN 0-9631981-0-6

Manufactured in the United States of America

Book design by Paula Thomson

*To those who took a step in faith,*
*sharing information, opinions, and wonderful stories.*
*Without you, my angels, these pages would not exist.*

*Farewell! I did not know thy worth,*
*But thou art gone, and now 'tis prized,*
*So angels walked unknown on earth,*
*But when they flew were recognized.*

THOMAS HOOD
*"TO AN ABSENTEE"*

# ACKNOWLEDGMENTS

Most books wouldn't be written without the help and encouragement of some wonderful people.

I am grateful for the professional advice and assistance of reference librarians, especially Marilyn Uselmann of the Arlington Heights Memorial Library, Thad Voss of Wheaton College, Theresa Bohm of Wycliffe Bible Translators, Dan Sharon of the Asher Library at Spertus College, and Harriet Leonard of the Duke University Divinity Library. I would also like to acknowledge the helpful research departments at the Christian Broadcasting Network, the Assemblies of God General Council Headquarters, and *Guideposts* magazine. The Reverend John H. Hampsch, C.M.F., Henrietta DePaepe, Pauline Cusack, and authors Charles and Frances Hunter deserve mention for providing me with valuable background material.

I extend special thanks to members of the clergy, including the Reverend John Lane, S.J., of Holy Family Church in Chicago; Dr. Timothy Warner, Trinity Evangelical Divinity School in Deerfield, Illinois; Pastor LaVerne Tucker, Redlands, California, and Rabbi Gedalia Schwartz of the Chicago Rabbinical Council.

Especially helpful were the people at the Loretto Chapel in Santa Fe, New Mexico; the 777th Precinct in Dayton, New Jersey; the Write to Publish Conference at Moody Bible Institute; the Swedenborg Foundation, and the National Centre for Padre Pio, as well as Fran White of the Guardian Angels.

My sister, Susan Fichter, merits special mention for being perhaps the first person to see a book possibility in all those letters.

## Acknowledgments

Grateful notice is due the magazine editors who printed my inquiries, most notably at *Liguorian, Our Sunday Visitor, Annals of St. Anne,* and *Sonlight/Sun,* as well as those lecture sponsors who allowed me to ask audiences for angel experiences.

Finally, I'd like to thank my wonderful husband and family and my friends, particularly members of the St. Theresa prayer group, the Hickory Nuts, and the St. Scholastica Class of '56 ...

... Your love through the years has sustained and blessed me.

*J. W. A.*
*Arlington Heights, Illinois*

# CONTENTS

# The Beginning...

*A guardian angel o'er his life presiding,*
*Doubling his pleasures, and his cares dividing.*
SAMUEL ROGERS
*"HUMAN LIFE"*

It was just past midnight on December 24, 1983. The Midwest was shivering through a record-breaking cold spell, complete with gale-force winds and frozen water pipes. And although our suburban Chicago household was filled with the snug sounds of a family at rest, I couldn't be a part of them, not until our twenty-one-year-old son pulled into the driveway. At the moment, Tim and his two roommates were driving home for Christmas, their first trip back since they had moved East last May. "Don't worry, Mom," Tim had reassured me over the phone last night. "We're going to leave before dawn tomorrow and drive straight through. We'll be fine!"

Kids. They do insane things. Under normal circumstances, I figured, a Connecticut-to-Illinois trek ought to take about eighteen hours. But the weather had turned so dangerously cold that radio reports warned against venturing outdoors, even for a few moments. And we had heard nothing from the travelers. Distressed, I pictured them on a desolate road. What if they ran into car problems or lost their way? And if they *had* been delayed, why hadn't Tim phoned?

Restlessly I paced and prayed in the familiar shorthand all mothers know: *God, send someone to help them.*

By now, as I later learned, the trio had stopped briefly in Fort Wayne, Indiana, to deposit Don at his family home. Common sense suggested that Tim and Jim stay the rest of the night and resume their trek in the morning. But when does common sense prevail with invincible young adults? There were only four driving hours left to reach home. And although it was the coldest night in Midwest history and the highways were snowy and deserted, the two had started out again.

They had been traveling for only a few miles on a rural access road to the Indiana tollway, when they noticed that the car's engine seemed sluggish, lurching erratically and dying to ten or fifteen miles per hour. Tim glanced uneasily at Jim. "Do not—" the radio announcer intoned, "—repeat— *do not* venture outside tonight, friends. There's a record windchill of eighty below zero, which means that exposed skin will freeze in less than a minute." The car surged suddenly, then coughed and slowed again.

"Tim," Jim spoke into the darkness, "we're not going to stall here, are we?"

"We can't," Tim answered grimly as he pumped the accelerator. "We'd die for sure."

But instead of picking up speed, the engine sputtered, chugging and slowing again. About a mile later, at the top of a small incline, the car crawled to a frozen stop.

Horrified, Tim and Jim looked at each other in the darkened interior. They could see across the fields in every direction, but, incredibly, theirs was the only vehicle in view. For the first time, they faced the fact that they were in enormous danger. There was no traffic, no refuge ahead, not even a farmhouse light blinking in the distance. It was as if they had landed on an alien, snow-covered planet.

And the appalling, unbelievable cold! Never in Tim's life had he experienced anything so intense. They couldn't run for help; he knew that now for sure. He and Jim were young and strong, but even if shelter was only a short distance away, they couldn't survive. The temperature would kill them in a matter of minutes.

"Someone will come along soon," Jim muttered, looking in every direction. "They're bound to."

"I don't think so," Tim said. "You heard the radio. Everyone in the world is inside tonight—except us."

"Then what are we going to do?"

"I don't know." Tim tried starting the engine again, but the ignition key clicked hopelessly in the silence. Bone-chilling cold had penetrated the car's interior, and his feet were already growing numb. *Well, God,* he prayed, echoing my own distant plea, *You're the only one who can help us now.*

It seemed impossible to stay awake much longer. . . . Then, as if they had already slipped into a dream, they saw headlights flashing at the car's left rear. But that was impossible. For they had seen no twin pinpricks of light in the distance, no hopeful approach. Where had the vehicle come from? Had they already died?

But no. For, miraculously, someone was knocking on the driver's side window. "Need to be pulled?" In disbelief they heard the muffled shout. But it was true. Their rescuer was driving a tow truck.

"Yes! Oh, yes, thanks!" Quickly, the two conferred as the driver, saying nothing more, drove around to the front of the car and attached chains. If there were no garages open at this hour, they would ask him to take them back to Don's house, where they could spend the rest of the night.

Swathed almost completely in a furry parka, hood and a scarf up to his eyes, the driver nodded at their request but said nothing more. He was calm, they noted as he climbed into his truck, seemingly unconcerned about the life-threatening circumstances in which he had found them. *Strange that he's not curious about us,* Tim mused, *and isn't even explaining where he came from or how he managed to approach without our seeing him. . . .* And had there been lettering on the side of the truck? Tim hadn't noticed any. *He's going to give us a big bill, on a night like this. I'll have to borrow some money from Don or his dad. . . .* But Tim was exhausted from the ordeal, and gradually, as he leaned against the seat, his thoughts slipped away.

They passed two locked service stations, stopped to alert Don from a pay phone, and were soon being towed back through the familiar Fort Wayne neighborhood. Hushed, Christmas lights long since extinguished and families asleep, Don's still seemed the most welcoming street they had ever been on. The driver maneuvered carefully around the cul-de-sac and pulled up in front of Don's house. Numb with cold, Tim and Jim raced to the side door where Don was waiting, then tumbled into the blessedly warm kitchen, safe at last.

Don slammed the door against the icy blast. "Hey, what happened?" he began, but Tim interrupted.

"The tow-truck driver, Don—I have to pay him. I need to borrow—"

"Wait a minute." Don frowned, looking past his friends through the window. "I don't see any tow truck out there."

Tim and Jim turned around. There, parked alone at the curb, was Tim's car. There had been no sound in the crystal-clear night of its release from the chains, no door slam, no chug of an engine pulling away. There had been no bill for Tim to pay, no receipt to sign, no farewell or "thank you" or "Merry Christmas...." Stunned, Tim raced back down the driveway to the curb, but there were no taillights disappearing in the distance, no engine noise echoing through the silent streets, nothing at all to mark the tow truck's presence.

Then Tim saw the tire tracks traced in the windblown snowdrifts. But there was only one set of marks ringing the cul-de-sac curve. And they belonged to Tim's car....

When Christmas carols fill the air and our worries regress in a temporary whirl of holiday nostalgia, everyone believes in angels. But it's harder to accept the likelihood that the "multitude of heavenly host" on that long-ago Bethlehem hillside has relevance in our lives too, that God's promise to send His angels to protect and rescue each of His children is a faithful pact, continuing for all eternity, throughout every season of the year.

Angels don't get much attention today. If the spirit world is acknowledged at all, it's usually the dark side, the bizarre satanic cults that are wreaking so much havoc, especially among our youth. Yet there is evidence that good spirits are also at work here on earth—combating evil, bringing news, warning us of danger, consoling us in our suffering...then vanishing, just as the angels did on that first Christmas night.

Angels don't submit to litmus tests, testify in court, or slide under a microscope for examination. Thus, their existence cannot be "proved" by the guidelines we humans usually use. To know one, perhaps, requires a willingness to suspend judgment, to open ourselves to possibilities we've only dreamed about. "The best and most beautiful things in the world cannot be seen or even touched," Helen Keller said. "They must be felt with the heart."

Was it an angel? Our family will never know for sure.

But on Christmas Eve in 1983, I heard the whisper of wings as a tow-truck driver answered a heavenly summons and brought our son safely home.

# Searching for Answers

*We not only live among men, but there are airy hosts, blessed spectators, sympathetic lookers-on, that see and know and appreciate our thoughts and feelings and acts.*

HENRY WARD BEECHER, *ROYAL TRUTHS*

*A*ngels. What did I really know about these celestial beings? As a Catholic, I was certainly aware of their existence. During childhood, I had learned a prayer to my guardian angel, and in college I had studied the hierarchy of angels, the nine choirs, each with its own function and assignment. But after Tim's curious rescue, I began to research angels with deeper interest.

One of the first facts I uncovered was a Gallup poll suggesting that more than sixty percent of Americans believe wholeheartedly in angels. Although scholars differ about specifics, their existence is accepted by all three of the great Western religions—Judaism, Christianity, and Islam. Angels are mentioned more than three hundred times in Sacred Scripture, acting alone or in great gatherings, carrying out God's commands, forming a heavenly court, and—significantly—protecting and bringing messages to people. They played crucial roles in the Old Testament, including the books of the Jewish Torah, and are cited frequently in the Islamic Koran. Socrates often asked his guardian angel for advice. Many famous saints, as well as Salvation Army founder General William Booth, claimed to have seen angels, and Abraham Lincoln said he felt their presence frequently. Celestial beings appear in the works of Dante, Milton, and Shakespeare, as well as in the works of contemporary authors.

As civilization evolved, so did humanity's understanding of angels. To early pagans, gods seemed either to be stars and planets or to dwell in the sky, so it was a simple transition to consider angels as winged spirits who could travel easily between heaven and earth.

Interpretations varied as time passed. Early Hebrews contended that the universe was a hierarchy, with God at the top and other entities radiating downward from Him. They believed that angels constitute the "court of heaven." In writings they referred to "the angels of God," and *bene Elohim*, "God's sons."

Christians believe that God made angels at or about the time He made the world (Saint Augustine thought the two acts of creation were simultaneous), but before He created human beings. They were given minds and wills, like us, but had no bodies. At some point, according to the Book of Revelations, some of the angels wished to be gods and there was a terrible battle in heaven. The defeated angels then became evil spirits, headed by Satan, who roam the world to this day. The Council of Nicaea in 325 declared *belief* in angels a dogma, but a later synod condemned the *worship* of angels.

Muslims also believe that angels were created before man. According to the Koran, when humans were fashioned as God's supreme handiwork, angels were required to bow down before them, an order that prompted Lucifer's rebellion. Before Muhammad united them under one religious banner of Islam, the Arabs had recognized many gods and goddesses and had seemed to include angels among them. Muhammad acknowledged Biblical writings, and thus included angels in his new religion. In fact, after being chosen as Prophet, Muhammad claimed to see a beautiful vision of Gabriel, who promised to guide him in his new role. Muslims believe that angels witness for or against people on the Day of Judgment, and that recording angels are present at prayer in the mosque and elsewhere.

My investigations revealed that, whatever their beginnings, angels have three basic purposes: to worship God, to serve as heralds between God and His people on earth, and to act as our caretakers, while never interfering with our free will. Saint Dionysius, Saint Paul, Pope Gregory, and others further divide angels into nine choirs, listed here in descending order, along with their main duties: Seraphim and Cherubim, who love and worship God; Thrones and Dominions, who regulate angelic duties; Virtues, who work miracles on earth; Powers, who protect us from demons; Principalities, Archangels, and Angels, who are ministers and guardians of people.

The four archangels best known to us are Raphael, Michael, Gabriel, and Uriel. Their numbers seem to be infinite, though, and throughout history, others have also been named. One of the oldest shrines in Turkey is dedicated to Michael, who is considered a great healer of the sick in that nation. Although angels are extremely powerful, they are, of course, subject to God in all things.

Religions differ on specifics about angels: For example, most Catholics believe that everyone receives a guardian angel at birth, a life companion especially suited to one's unique personality. Catholic children learn a comforting little prayer to initiate "conversation" with their angel, and the feast day of guardian angels is celebrated on October second. Ancient Jewish angelology also taught the personal-angel theory. In fact, the Talmud speaks of every Jew being assigned eleven thousand guardian angels at birth! The various Protestant faiths hold divergent views, most believing that we shouldn't pray to angels, but that we may ask them to intervene for us.

As angels began to appear in art, around the fourth century, artists gave them wings in order to distinguish them from the apostles or other holy men and women. We also think of them as dimpled cherubs, or perhaps a white-garbed chorus, as on that first Christmas night. Survivors of near-death experiences, however, cite "bright beings of light" that they met along the way—a reminder that light, symbolized in artists' renditions by halos or luminous bodies, represents heaven and, perhaps, those occupying it.

In Scripture, many angels appear as powerful, fearless soldiers. But there are also Bible stories about men and women meeting angels in human form, angels who look just like ordinary mortals...actually, just like Tim's angel. The companion in the Book of Tobit and the strangers who visit Lot in Genesis are good examples. And did not Saint Paul admonish the Hebrews—and all who would come after them—to "show hospitality, for by that means some have entertained angels without knowing it"?

The more I read, the more I realized that far from being outdated, angels are part of today's world too. There are cities, sports teams, aviator groups, and charitable activities named after angels. Members of the national street safety patrol known as the Guardian Angels wear T-shirts with an emblem featuring an eye, wings, and a shield denoting, according to founder and director Curtis Sliwa, "angellike protection offered to everyone, even those who don't want us looking out for them." There is an Angel Collectors Club of America, a national association of angel lovers with its own newsletter and annual convention. Angel Threads, a children's boutique, operates in Tucson. There is an Angels in Heaven day nursery in Cleveland and an angel collectible mail-order business in Riverside, California. Toller Cranston lives in a Toronto house filled with angel paintings, mobiles, and other celestial art; this six-time Canadian figure-skating champion likes angels because, he says, "they can leave gravity behind."

Even Hollywood gets into the angel act on occasion. Who can forget Clarence in the movie *It's a Wonderful Life*, a lovable, bumbling angel who shows a suicidal man (James Stewart) the value of his life and what would have happened if he had not been true to his principles? Stewart has always maintained that the role was his favorite. *Field of Dreams*, while not specifically about angel spirits, made such an impact on moviegoers that the baseball field in Iowa where it was filmed still attracts thousands of tourists every year.

And consider the popular television series *Highway to Heaven*, produced by the late Michael Landon. Landon played the role of an angel, Jonathan Smith, sent from heaven to persuade hurting people to help one another. The idea had come to Landon one day while, stuck in traffic on a Los Angeles freeway, he watched drivers angrily honk and yell at one another. If they used even a fraction of that energy on being kind, Landon mused, how the world could be changed! Soon he developed a series based on the idea that kindness, not anger, solves problems, with the central character an angel who could make mistakes but could also be a spiritual catalyst in people's lives.

But Hollywood is fiction. Were *real* angels still around today, still ministering to us by caress, whisper—or in human form? If this dramatic, unexpected, and marvelously loving rescue had happened to my son, would I find that others had similar stories? It seemed logical; since I believe God loves all His children with equal intensity, He would certainly extend to everyone the same protection He had provided for Tim. But maybe few of us recognized this help when it came. Or perhaps we passed such moments off as "lucky breaks" or "coincidence." I would have to dig deeper to find the answers.

But it was one thing to read privately about angels, quite another to ask someone, even a close friend, "Have you ever met an angel?" People vary in their willingness to trust the supernatural, I think. Many consider the idea of heavenly beings walking around helping humans as incomprehensible. We are, after all, creatures of the twentieth century's "theology" of scientific proof. Others agree that such an encounter might occur, that we live in a world where not everything is explainable in logical terms, but they maintain that real miracles wouldn't—*couldn't*—happen to *them*. After all, didn't one have to be exceptionally pious in order to qualify? And if I found people who had had an encounter similar to Tim's, would they be willing to share it?

Taking a deep breath, I went to the post office and rented a box. Then I wrote to magazines where readers were familiar with my byline and asked that my letter be published: *I am looking for people who believe they may have met an angel,* I wrote. *I am not talking about human beings who, because of kindly deeds, might rightfully be called "angels." I am talking about spirits who appeared in human form to give some kind of help. Please write to me at this box number....*

A few of the magazine editors wrote back stating that they didn't publish letters of this kind. They either objected to having their pages used as a means of research or, I suspect, considered my request a bit too weird. From others, I received no acknowledgment. This could mean a decision to discard my letter—or publish it. But even if my request was honored, what if no one responded? What if readers laughed or, worse, said to one another, "That Joan Anderson used to be a nice, normal writer. But I think she's gone round the bend, don't you?"?

I waited, kept looking for angel material, and, one day, saw one of my requests in print. A few weeks later I went to the post office, inserted my key into my rented box and gathered my courage. This was probably what people call "the moment of truth." Today I would discover whether Tim's event was an isolated occurrence—or whether we were members of a great and glorious community of people whose lives had been touched by a heavenly being.

I swung open the mailbox door—and stepped back in amazement. It was filled with envelopes.

# "Angels All Around Us"

Yet many will not believe there is any such thing as
a sympathy of souls.
ISAAK WALTON, *LIFE OF DR. DONNE*

"*I* haven't told this to many people. I guess I'm
afraid my family or friends would laugh, or think I
was having hallucinations...."

"*If I try to explain what I saw, he gives me That
Look, as if he thinks I need counseling....*"

"*It all happened so fast that I didn't consider angelic intervention, not until days later. Then I started
putting the pieces together....*"

The letters were a joy to read. In subsequent months, as
other magazines printed my invitation—and I developed
enough courage to request stories from audiences at my humor speeches and writers' conferences—many strangers
shared their "special event" with me. I also corresponded
with some authors of angel books already in print, to ask for
their insights or to request addresses of people they had in-
terviewed. My files began to grow.

I found it fascinating that, although angel incidents varied, the *reaction* of those involved was almost always the
same, and twofold: first, a hesitancy about sharing; then,

once that was overcome, an awe that, even years later, was still powerfully aroused by the memory of the incident.

The reluctance to go public was understandable. Like those who had experienced clinical death, had been revived, and had attempted to tell others what they'd seen, my interviewees had often felt rejected. Gradually, they had learned to ponder such happenings silently, lest their wonder be diminished by the disbelief of others. None wanted to lose that precious conviction that they had been especially blessed, permitted—just for a moment—to look into a world they must usually accept on faith.

The emotional response seemed universal too. One middle-aged woman, talking to me on a stairway during a break in a writers' conference, described a scene from her childhood. Piqued at some trivial matter, she had run off into the woods and had promptly gotten lost. She kept walking as the sky darkened, and was horrified to come across her own footprints; she'd been walking in a circle. Suddenly, she felt a gentle hand on her brow, and a tender inner voice told her to "go straight ahead." Immediately she obeyed, and in less than a mile, she saw her house on the horizon.

"It's been forty-five years, but I can still feel that hand and hear that wonderful voice," she said, eyes misting as she swallowed hard and stared over my head into a place I could not follow. Others choked up on the telephone when attempting to describe what they had seen or heard. Though none could fully explain, all seemed transformed in the light of their encounter.

As I separated and categorized the responses, I noticed that they fell into one of several groups. Like the lady in the woods, there were those who hadn't met an angel in human form but had seen lights, heard a voice, or felt a touch.

Others mentioned their awareness of a "presence" during significant moments, as if special friends had come to share the occasion.

"I was visiting my neighbor in the hospital," one told me, "and suddenly I felt the company of angels all around us. 'Oh! There are angels here!' I said, before I could help myself. The patient and her sister seemed surprised, but willing to accept my notion.

"The next morning my neighbor died, and later her sister told me what a comfort it was to know that angels had been in the room with us. It's been forty years, and I've never had a similar experience, but I still remember that indescribable feeling."

Many letters involved deathbeds, where those keeping vigil saw a radiance on the face of the dying one, or heard him speak to someone unknown just before closing his eyes for the last time.

"Look, Mother, there are angels all around us, and one is more beautiful than the rest," one eleven-year-old said as he was dying from peritonitis.

"I can't see them, Joey," his mother answered. Thinking her son was delirious, she tried to soothe him, but Joseph was insistent.

"See, they're right here, so close I could touch them," he told her again. Joseph's grieving mother was struck by her son's attitude of profound joy and peace. It became a consolation to the entire family.

F. S. Smythe, who attempted to climb Mount Everest in 1933, wrote of the same "friendly presence" in his account of the expedition. "A strange feeling possessed me that I was accompanied by another. In its company I could not feel lonely, nor could I come to any harm. It was always there to sustain me on my solitary climb up the snow-covered slabs. [When] I halted and extracted some mint cake from my pocket, it was so near and so strong that instinctively I divided the mint into two halves and turned round with one half in my hand to offer it to my companion."[1]

Another respondent told me of a time when she was seventeen and, for several nights in a row, felt a presence at the foot of her bed. "I didn't actually see anything," she explained. "It was more the kind of feeling you get when you're aware of someone looking at you when you're in traffic, or reading, or sitting with your back to a doorway."

She sensed that there were two angels standing side by side, facing her. Their mission seemed to be one of simple reassurance, and the young girl felt warm, sheltered, and at peace. The following years were turbulent. "But knowing that two angels had guarded me for those nights—and were probably still nearby—kept me from doubting a loving God."

Theologians maintain that although angels can and do appear as humans, their image is not necessary for their presence to be there; God and His messengers are just as close to those who do *not* see them as to those who do. Certainly there must be times when we never realize that an angel ministered to us. We feel a nudge, a mysterious urge to do something a bit out of character. Or something is, oddly, taken care of for us. Perhaps a sudden flash of insight is actually a spirit interceding to keep us safe and healthy. "An angel reaches down and gives us a heavenly hug, and we say, 'What a glorious day!'" wrote one believer.

Another group of correspondents did not see anyone protecting them—but others around them did. One reader sent me the well-documented story of Alice Z., a young Seventh-Day Adventist selling literature door-to-door in a hostile neighborhood in the Philippines. Alice was welcomed into a house where, curiously, the guard dogs seemed friendly rather than fierce. *Two* chairs were set for her rather than one, and the lady of the house addressed the second chair as if someone were there, and she remarked to Alice that her "companion" certainly looked becoming in white.[2] I found similar episodes where the protected one, like Alice, had no awareness that anyone was there, but the witnesses—all credible and normal—insisted they were seeing people.

The majority of my correspondents told of meeting angels in human form. Some offered messages; others rescued the person from tricky or dangerous situations. Most often these visitors were of few words—they did their jobs, then left. Occasionally, there was something otherworldly about the experience as it was happening, and the person recognized the being as an angel.

For example, preacher John Weaver and some companions had gone hunting for elk in Montana. John was about two-thirds of the way up a ridge when he saw a man coming out of the trees on the next hill. The stranger wasn't wearing hunter orange or carrying a rifle, and though he seemed to be walking at a normal pace, he covered the distance so quickly that it seemed like a matter of seconds.

And he left no footprints in the snow.

"The man walked up to me and shook my hand. 'John, do you know who I am?' he asked me."

And Weaver did, through the enlightened eyes of faith. The man was the same being who had helped John some twenty years before when his car broke down.

The two sat on some rocks, discussed John's current ministry and his needs—just like two friends—and the angel-visitor left, after reassuring Weaver of God's love and faithfulness.[3]

In this case, because of the footprint phenomenon and the immediate spiritual recognition, Weaver knew his visitor was an angel. For most of my correspondents, however, the encounters were so conventional that it was only later that they began to wonder. "It seemed just too coincidental..." or "It took a while before I realized how odd it all was..." were classic comments. Because such "visitors" came in human form, initially it was easy to explain them away.

This was not new, I discovered. Throughout time, angels have typically appeared in whatever form the visited person was most willing to accept—perhaps a winged version for children, or a benign grandfatherly type for a woman in distress. I found reports of angels speaking in familiar dialects or assuming the same race as the visited one. "Angels, and angels alone, are minds without bodies," observes philosopher Mortimer J. Adler in *The Angels and Us* (New York: Macmillan, 1982). "Therein lies their fascination [in that] when they assume bodies, they do so only for the sake of engaging in their earthly ministry."

Nor did it seem to matter—at least to my correspondents—whether they *knew* their helper was an angel; one's recognition or faith wasn't a prerequisite for aid. But there does seem to be one common denominator: Author and angel scholar Betty Malz notes that angelic protection never seems to occur when people are *deliberately* breaking the laws of society or even the natural law—for example, taking risks by speeding down a highway, or stealing from or abusing others. Following one's own headstrong will or charging into danger and waiting for God to rescue us, says Malz, apparently moves us out of the "safety zone" in which angels operate. She and others believe, however, that people can intercede for us and perhaps summon spiritual help.

Many of these stories confirm Malz's observation: Contributors were asking for assistance or somehow "tuned in" to the heavenly realm when help occurred. Some suggested a similar theory: Unless we *deliberately* invoke their aid, angels can help only in a limited way.

Finally, a small group of my letter-writers reported seeing a real angel, that is, a being that *looked* the way we all assume angels look. "How can you be sure they aren't...you know...kooks?" my hairstylist once asked while, over a trim, I told her about my project. I couldn't, actually. And it would probably take faith on anyone's part to accept their stories.

But, once again, these people didn't *care* whether anyone believed them. Their conviction was powerful in its simplicity. "I know what I saw—and it changed my life," one woman said quietly. That seemed to be enough.

I had started collecting stories because of Tim's experience. Now I found myself with bulging folders that I took along to read while waiting in a dentist's office or riding on the train. The letters deserved a wider audience. I selected several of the most intriguing, and began to write a book.

What has this quest taught me? I used to think that angels were minor adjuncts in the spiritual world and that dwelling on them could only distract us from God. But today I believe that angels help us lift our souls heavenward, to Him. Throughout time they have been part of the Divine plan, so it seems God wants us to know about them and to feel free to ask them for protection for ourselves or loved ones. The subject of angels requires a great deal of discernment and respect. Angels must be treated not as a curiosity, but as an entity from which we can learn, and receive, much. In short, they can become our dear and loving companions ...if we are willing to allow them into our lives.

"There is a diversity of angel forms to be celebrated, and there is an element of surprise to be realized," writes G. Don Gilmore in *Angels, Angels Everywhere*, "but unless people revive their childlike wonder and imagination, they may never experience such things."

Jesus put it another way: "Unless you become as little children, you cannot enter heaven." He was speaking of the trust, the wonder, the innocent acceptance of things not provable...in short, he was speaking of faith. "Blessed is he that has not seen, and has believed."

The people who have shared their experiences in this book all suspect they have been touched by the same spiritual messengers who graced the world at its beginning—the only thing that has changed is the setting. And they are left with a sense of indescribable wonder and the warm assurance that, whatever their failings, God is holding them gently in the palm of His hand.

As the saying goes, to those who are willing to believe, no explanation of the events on the following pages is necessary. To those who are not willing to believe, no explanation is possible.

Was it an angel? It's up to you.

# Angel in the Cockpit

*How sweetly did they float upon the wings*
*Of silence through the empty-vaulted night...*
                                    MILTON, *COMUS*

David Moore and his wife, Florence, discovered in July 1971 that Florence's mother was dying of cancer. The Moores lived in the small town of Yoakum, Texas, then, but they began driving back and forth to Hendersonville, North Carolina, to visit the sick woman. After one trip, David decided to leave the car in North Carolina for Florence to use, and take the bus back to Texas.

"It was the worst idea I ever had," he says, laughing. "Forty-six hours of riding and listening to babies cry! On our budget I couldn't afford to fly, but I made a vow to walk if I had to—anything to avoid getting on another bus!"

The following week, as David packed and planned a hitchhiking route to Hendersonville, Henry Gardner phoned. Henry had heard about David's transportation problems, and he volunteered to fly David to North Carolina in his small Cessna 180 and get in some sight-seeing at the same time. David accepted gratefully.

David had never flown in a small plane, and he was nervous as the two men taxied down the runway early the next morning. But the little aircraft lifted gracefully, and he sat back to handle his unfamiliar duties as navigator. Within a half hour, however, as they neared Houston, they ran into fog.

"This is no problem," Henry reassured an increasingly nervous David. "We have aviation maps on board, and look—you can see the Houston radio towers rising above the fog. All we have to do is watch the towers, and we can tell where we are."

He was right, and their journey continued. But the fog worsened, and just outside Jackson, Mississippi, the plane's radio and instruments died. Now the pair couldn't see anything on the ground, nor could they talk to people in the control tower.

Just as David was becoming desperate, the fog lifted for a moment to reveal the airport directly beneath them. Henry took the plane down smoothly, and within minutes they had found an airport mechanic. Relieved, the two men grabbed a quick lunch and were soon airborne, with instruments and radio restored and fuel tanks filled.

Everything went smoothly for a while. The sun had come out, and David's tension diminished. He began to enjoy the flight and his bird's-eye view of the ground. As they traveled northeast, he could see Atlanta off to his right. "I was getting excited," David says, "knowing that soon I would be with my wife and daughter again."

But as the plane passed Greenville, South Carolina, the fog, which had been patchy and broken, turned once again into a continuous gray mass. There was enough visibility for Henry to clear the first mountain range, but as the two looked into the distance, they saw a solid wall of fog, and their hearts sank. Henry radioed Asheville Airport for instructions.

"Our field is closed because of fog," the air-traffic controller responded, "and we have no capability for instrument landing. Return to Greenville and land there."

"But I can't," Henry protested. "We're almost out of fuel—we won't have enough to fly back to Greenville."

There was a silence. Then, "Okay," the radio voice snapped. "We'll get the ground crew ready. Come in on an emergency landing."

David gripped the sides of his seat. They seemed to be flying in a dense gray blanket, and the Asheville control tower couldn't possibly see them. How were he and Henry going to land? "We can use the aviation maps, just like we did before," Henry reassured David, and after a brief scan of the blueprint, he began his blind descent. The airport runway *should* be beneath them—but what if it wasn't?

Suddenly a voice came over the radio: "Pull it up! Pull it up!"

Henry immediately pulled up on the stick. As he did so, the men saw a split in the fog, and the view beneath sent tremors of fear through each of them. Instead of being over the runway, they were above an interstate highway! Had they descended a few feet farther, they would have hit a bridge and certainly crashed.

The two looked at each other. They were almost out of fuel, and inside the grayness it was impossible to know where they were. Henry tried to descend again, but almost hit the tips of some trees poking above the fog. Again, he pulled up sharply. There seemed to be no way out of their dilemma. Without enough fuel—or guidance from the control tower—how could they possibly land?

Then, with enormous relief, they heard the controller's composed voice breaking into the tense silence in the cockpit. "If you will listen to me," he said, "I'll help you get down."

"Go ahead," Henry radioed back in relief.

The controller began his instructions. "Come down just a little," he said. "Now over to the right. Down a little more...."

David gripped the seat, praying intently. Thank God the controller had been able to pick them up on radar, despite the airport's apparent lack of the necessary instruments. But would they make it in time? It seemed impossible. The fuel needle hovered on *E*, but the voice went on with calm authority: "Not so fast. Easy, easy now...." Was this nightmare flight ever going to end? And would he see his wife and daughter again?

"Raise it up a little now. No, you're too far left." The journey seemed to be taking forever. But all of a sudden the controller said, "You're right over the end of the runway. Set it down...now!"

Obediently, Henry dropped the plane through the fog, and the two men recognized the beginning of a runway just ahead, with lights along both sides. It was the most welcome sight they had ever seen. Within minutes, they had touched down. Tears of gratitude and relief filled David's eyes when he saw Florence standing at the end of the runway.

The plane taxied to a stop, and the two men offered a quick prayer of thanksgiving. Then Henry turned the radio on again. "Thanks so much," he told the air-traffic controller, his voice shaky with relief. "You probably saved our lives."

But the controller's response stopped both men in their tracks. "What are you talking about? We lost all radio contact with you when we told you to return to Greenville."

"You *what?*" Henry asked, incredulous.

"We never heard from you again, and we never heard you talking to us or to anyone else," the controller told them. "We were stunned when we saw you break through the clouds."

David and Henry looked at each other. Who had guided them through the grayness and onto safe ground? They would never know for sure. But even today David never hears a small airplane without thinking of that flight. "I know now that, insignificant as I may be in this big world, God always has His eye on me," he says. "He sustains me through the storm and the fog."

# Night Guide

*We are like children, who stand in need of masters to enlighten us and direct us; and God has provided for this, by appointing his angels to be our teachers and guides.*

SAINT THOMAS AQUINAS

*W*illiam and Virginia Jackson, native New Englanders, have lived in Florida for several years. Virginia often asks her angel's help. Once, the couple drove from Las Vegas to El Paso through Death Valley—and only later discovered that their car's fan belt hadn't been functioning at all. How had they managed to cross a treacherous desert without a vital piece of engine equipment? Virginia believes they were protected by spiritual beings.

But it was during another journey, about six years ago, that angelic guardianship seemed especially vivid. The Jacksons had visited their daughter in Hudson and were driving home on a Sunday evening. "We try never to travel then, because in the area where we live, everything is closed and deserted," Virginia says. "If you get in trouble on the road, there's no place to go for help."

They had covered only a small distance when their car headlights went out. What to do? William pulled over, raised the hood and looked hopefully down the road. Virginia started to pray.

Almost immediately a policeman drove up. "Do you know of a garage open on Sunday nights around here?" William asked.

The trooper thought a minute. "There may be one. Why don't you put your hazard lights on and follow me?"

The Jacksons did so, but the garage was closed. Since they lived in a neighboring county, the policeman wasn't able to leave his route and escort them farther. Instead, he led them to Route 41. "Park here along the road," he suggested. "Someone's bound to come along who can guide you closer to where you live."

As the policeman was speaking, a car pulled up ahead, and William and the policeman went over to talk to the driver.

"Aren't we fortunate?" William said to Virginia as he got back into the car and the policeman drove off. "That fellow ahead is driving right past our town. He'll go slowly, and I told him when we get to Route 44, we'll turn off. What luck, out here, to find someone going in our direction!"

Virginia was not so sure it was luck. She kept praying.

The couple honked as they reached their exit, and the good samaritan ahead waved and drove on. Now the Jacksons crawled to the Mid-State Bank, right in the center of their deserted town. They were only a few miles from home, but the dark drive would be extremely dangerous without lights.

"Why don't we sit here for a while, in case someone we know drives by?" Virginia suggested.

A few minutes passed. Then a red car approached. Instead of parking or leaning out the window to inquire about them, the driver, an indistinguishable figure in the darkened interior, slowed down and pulled in front of the Jacksons. In the bank's parking-lot lights, Virginia could see the first few digits on the car's license plate, and they seemed familiar.

"I think that's someone we know," she told William.

"Well, he seems to be waiting for us to follow him." William started the car and eased behind the stranger, who pulled away very slowly.

The last leg of the Jacksons' journey was almost over. What a relief. It could have been so dangerous, and yet they had been protected every inch of the way. Virginia continued to look at the car in front of them as they drove. Although she couldn't see the driver, she was able to read, a little at a time, the remaining digits on the license plate. "Oh, I know who that is!" she finally told William. "I recognize the number. That car sits in a driveway a block from our house. I pass it all the time—no wonder it seemed familiar."

Sure enough, when the driver approached that house, he tooted and turned into the driveway. William and Virginia waved their thanks, then went on to their own house, glad to relax after their ordeal.

The next day they decided to thank the driver personally, and they walked down to the house. The same red car, with the same license plate, stood in the driveway where they had watched it turn in last night.

A woman answered their knock, and as the Jacksons offered their thanks, she grew more and more mystified. "I wasn't out at all last night," she protested. "I never drive at night."

"Then it was your husband," Virginia concluded.

"That's impossible," the woman said. "My husband couldn't have led you home."

"Oh, but he did," Virginia said. "Without his help, we'd probably still be parked at the bank. I saw your license-plate number. And that red car definitely turned into this drive-way."

The woman shook her head. "You don't understand," she told Virginia. "I'm the only driver, and I haven't moved the car in several days. It couldn't have been my husband. He doesn't drive anymore. You see, he's blind."

The Jacksons later discovered that the man in the house was indeed blind. And for some time, whenever Virginia met her, the woman would give Virginia a look as if to say, "What kind of hallucination have you had today?"

The couple has puzzled over their rescue since then. But however it happened, one thing is certain. "I was praying for help during the whole journey," Virginia sums it up. "Why should I be surprised that we received it?"

# Invisible Intervention

*The angel of the lord encamps around those who fear him, and he delivers them.*

PSALMS 34:7

Corrie ten Boom was a middle aged spinster who led an uneventful life as a watchmaker in Haarlem, Holland. When Hitler's armies conquered much of Europe in the early 1940s, Corrie's brother, a minister in the Dutch Reformed Church, began to shelter Jewish refugees. Eventually, as German troops occupied Holland, Corrie decided to help too, by hiding Jewish friends in a secret passage within her home until they could be smuggled out of the country.

Gradually, the ten Boom household became the center of the city's resistance movement, with hundreds of Jews passing through, and some being hidden permanently. "My room resembled a beehive, a sort of clearing house for supply and demand," she wrote in *A Prisoner, and Yet* ... [4]

On February 28, 1944, Corrie, her sister, Betsie, and their father were betrayed and arrested. Although the Gestapo searched their house, the secret room had been so cleverly designed that they could find no evidence of smuggling. Since the ten Booms refused to reveal the house's hiding place, they were convicted of stealing food-ration cards, and sent to prison. (All but one of their guests ultimately reached safety.)

Corrie's father lived for only ten days after being sentenced, but for Corrie and Betsie, the next year was hell itself. And yet through her indomitable spirit and firm faith in God, Corrie brought hope and kindness to many suffering prisoners. To her knowledge, she never saw an angel "in the flesh," but she found evidence of angelic intervention.

At one point, as she and other inmates arrived at the dreaded Ravensbrueck, a women's extermination camp, Corrie realized in horror that all their possessions, including warm clothes, were being taken from them. They would freeze in this desolate wasteland. And what of her little Bible? She wore it on a string around her neck, and it had been her consolation through the desolate days thus far. But surely it would be confiscated.

Before it was Corrie's turn to be stripped and searched, she asked permission to use the bathroom. There she wrapped the Bible in Betsie's and her woolen underwear, laid the bundle in a corner, and returned to the row of waiting prisoners. Later, after Corrie and Betsie had been redressed in the prison's regulation undershirt and dress, Corrie hid the roll of warm underwear and her Bible under her clothes. It bulged considerably, but she prayed, *Lord, send Your angels to surround me.*

Then, realizing that angels were spirits, she amended the prayer: *Lord, don't let them be transparent today, for the guards must not see me!*

Calmly, she then passed the guards. Everyone else in line was searched from side to side and top to bottom, every bulge and crease investigated. The woman in front of Corrie had hidden a woolen vest under her dress, and it was immediately spotted and confiscated. Behind her, Betsie was searched.

But Corrie passed without being touched—or even looked at—by anyone. It was as if no one saw her in line. At the outer door, as a second row of guards felt the body of each prisoner, she was again unnoticed.

Bibles were forbidden property. To be found with one meant a doubling of the prison sentence as well as a cutback on rations, which were already just above starvation level. Corrie lived for several months at this cruelest of institutions and was subjected to many searches. She and Betsie also conducted clandestine worship services and Bible study for inmates of all faiths and nationalities. But there seemed to be an invisible wall of protection around her Bible, for the guards never found it.

In Ravensbrueck, prisoners had to surrender most medicines, but they were allowed to keep a few toilet articles. Corrie kept a bottle of Davitamon, a liquid vitamin compound, that, at the time she entered Ravensbrueck, was about half full.

Vitamin deficiency was one of the worst hazards to prisoners, and Corrie's instinct was to hoard the precious vial for Betsie, who by now was emaciated and ill. But the others were sick too, "and it was hard to say 'no' to eyes that burned with fever, hands that shook with chill," she wrote in *The Hiding Place*.[5] Soon the number receiving a daily dose was over thirty, and still, "every time I tilted the little bottle, a drop appeared at the top of the stopper. Many times I lay awake trying to fathom the marvel of supply lavished upon us." Although she could not understand how it was happening, the drops kept coming.

One day someone who worked in the prison hospital

smuggled a yeast bag containing vitamins to Corrie, asking that she dispense them to as many prisoners as possible. Corrie gave each woman enough to last her for a week. But when she opened her own little bottle of Davitamon, the bottle was dry. However, the yeast bag took its place, continuing to yield vitamins for many weeks. Corrie always believed that angels had a hand in these unaccountable events.

Betsie died in prison from starvation and illness. A short time later, Corrie was called into the warden's office and released. Her suffering had ended. But life would never again be the same.

Corrie began a new career, opening homes for people who had been damaged by brutal treatment during the war, places where they could heal their bodies and minds. To support her homes, she went around the world giving lectures. It was not until 1959, however, that Corrie discovered the most significant "invisible intervention" she had received. She was revisiting Ravensbrueck as part of a pilgrimage honoring the ninety-six thousand women who died there, when she learned that her own release had been the result of a "clerical error." A week after she'd been granted freedom, all the women prisoners her age had been taken to the gas chambers.

# Neither Wind nor Rain...

*Millions of spiritual creatures walk the earth,*
*Unseen, both when we wake and when we sleep...*
                                       MILTON, *PARADISE LOST*

If Corrie ten Boom's angels encamped around her to make her invisible, what else can a ring of determined protective spirits do for us? I found the story of a couple who were staying at a hotel when a fire broke out. It was two-thirty A.M., and the hall was full of flames. At first, the couple believed they were doomed. But the husband called upon God for help, picked up his wife, and ran down the hall. The flames and smoke seemed to roll back, he said, until they reached the safety of the lobby.[6]

Another woman wrote of a time when, just divorced, heartsick and praying for help, she drove her truck through a driving rainstorm. Her son was the first to notice that the rain wasn't hitting their truck. In the side and rearview mirrors, they could see the deluge beating down, flattening foliage, pelting houses and barns. But their windshield, without wipers, was perfectly clear! This tender gesture lifted the woman's spirits and gave her courage for the difficult road that lay ahead.[7]

Lucille Johnson, a teacher, believes she experienced an "encampment" too. In 1949, a polio epidemic swept through the area of Iowa where Lucille taught, and she contracted the disease, probably from her students.

"I was hospitalized for over six months, and finally 'graduated' with two sawed-off crutches with arm supports called 'Kenny sticks,'" Lucille told me. "I went back to college to finish my degree, then taught again." Through her career, her marriage, and the birth of her daughter, Lucille managed to get around first with two crutches, then with one, and finally, "due to vanity," she says, without any prop.

But polio left her with a weak right side. In order to support her body, she still must lock her knee when she walks, and these days she usually uses a cane. "I fall very easily, and I once broke a kneecap," she explains. "High and gusty winds are especially dangerous, as they thrust me off balance. Even when I was much younger, I avoided going shopping in downtown Davenport because when that famous Iowa wind blew, I could hardly manage to cross the street without being pushed over!"

In 1977, Lucille and her family built a house near New Salisbury, Indiana, and Lucille got involved in St. Michael's congregation. As their first Christmas in the new house approached, Lucille decided to thank God for her blessings by attending mass every day during December.

Each day of the first week, Lucille drove the seven miles to St. Michael's. But on Monday morning of the second week, she awakened to the sound of her nemesis, wind. Weather reports warned of extreme gusts, a condition that could topple Lucille and severely injure her. Should she take the risk? *God,* she prayed, *I know I promised You...and I'll do my part.*

Cautiously, Lucille drove to St. Michael's. The wind pushed and bounced her car the whole way, but it was especially nerve-racking whenever she came to a clearing or unprotected area and the vehicle shuddered like a toy that could easily be tossed. Exhausted from gripping the steering wheel and riding the brake, Lucille finally parked about a half block away from the church entrance and looked around hopefully. Was anyone approaching, someone with a strong arm who wouldn't mind letting her hang on?

No. She seemed alone, and she almost decided to turn back. The wind sounded as though it was rising and, even parked, her little car bucked and quivered. But she had come this far in safety.... Reluctantly she opened the door and stepped out into the turmoil.

Strangely, the wind seemed to have suddenly died, for she felt nothing at all. "I was expecting to be blown nearly off my feet," Lucille says, "but to my surprise, I didn't feel the slightest puff, not even a breeze. There didn't seem to be any air moving at all." God had apparently heard her prayer and calmed the wind for her. *What a loving Father!* she thought.

Only.... Puzzled, Lucille looked up at the trees in the churchyard. Far from being motionless, they were swaying wildly, and she could actually hear the branches creak with the strain. But Lucille *felt* nothing, not even a slight current to ruffle her hair. How could this be?

She didn't know, but she began the walk to the church doors with growing confidence. The wind was probably blowing high and not low, she decided. If that was possible, it would explain the phenomenon. And yet.... She stopped in amazement again. Rushing past her in a whirlpool of motion were several dead brown leaves, obviously propelled by a force that was ground level, yet not touching her at all.

Lucille climbed the cracked church steps one at a time, holding on tightly to the iron railing and forcing her body up with her left arm. But again, no wind fought her. Reaching the top, she pulled open the heavy door with ease and stepped inside, the door swinging slowly closed. But not quite.

Caught by a powerful draft, the door began to fly back open. Lucille caught it and felt the terrible force as the gust fought her. As she struggled to pull the door shut, a friend grabbed the other side and half plunged inside. "This is the worst gale I've ever felt!" she exclaimed to Lucille, then looked at her more closely. "Why, you're not even rumpled!" she said. "Didn't you just come in?"

"She was right. My hair was not tossed or tumbled, nor were my clothes in any kind of disorder," Lucille reports. "I was completely calm and unruffled, even though a storm continued to rage outside."

Lucille will never know for sure if an encampment of angels threw rings of protection around her, rings that even gale-force winds could not penetrate. But although the presence of angels is perhaps more difficult to grasp than the wind itself, many believe it is entirely possible.

# The Safety Inspector

*An angel! Or if not, an earthly paragon!*
SHAKESPEARE, *CYMBELINE*

Jean Hannan Ondracek of Omaha was one of the first to answer my request for angel stories. Hers is a memory treasured ever since it happened in 1958.

Jean had gone to a spa in the Ozarks with her sister Pat and two girlfriends, young adults enjoying a weekend of sunning and fun. Because Jean was the only one who knew how to swim, she decided on Saturday morning to venture into the lake. Her companions planned to stay on shore and work on their tans. "There were other people in the area," Jean remembers, "but no one very close to our spot on the shore. There were no lifeguards patrolling this section of beach. As far as I knew, I was the only swimmer in the lake."

The sun was warm, the water refreshing, and time—and distance—passed more quickly than Jean had anticipated. At a point much farther from shore than she had thought—and where the lake was quite deep—Jean suddenly ran out of breath. Shocked, she realized that she did not have enough energy to get herself back to shore.

She called and waved frantically, but she could hardly make out the tiny figures on the sand. And no one was looking her way. As her fear increased, Jean realized that she could drown. "God, help me! Help me!" she prayed aloud.

Suddenly she saw something bobbing in the water to her left. A boat! It looked like an old abandoned canoe. If she could get to it, perhaps she could row it back.... With the last of her energy, Jean paddled over to the boat, but her heart sank when she saw it. It was old, all right, without oars, and apparently chained or anchored in some way to something at the bottom of the lake. She could hold on for a moment, steady herself and catch her breath, and that was surely a blessing. But the respite was at best temporary.

How long could she hang on before Pat and the others noticed her absence? Or would they simply assume she had come ashore on another stretch of beach, and not put out any alarm for her? What would happen when the sun's rays began to burn her, or she became thirsty, or her arms, clutching to the slippery sides, became tired? What if the old boat splintered under her weight? Jean started to cry. "Help!" she called again. "Somebody, help!"

To her right, Jean suddenly heard splashing. She turned to see a man a few years older than she gliding easily through the waves, then treading water in front of her. "Hi," he greeted her calmly, as if it were the most natural thing in the world to be passing by. "Having trouble?"

"I—I'm out of breath and can't get back," she answered, relief flooding her. "Where did you come from? I didn't see anyone swimming—and I was certainly looking for help!"

The young man shrugged casually. "Oh, I'm a safety inspector, and one of my jobs is saving lives in water, if I have to. Do you think you can swim back?"

"Oh, no." Jean shook her head. "I'm exhausted."

"Come on, you can do it!" The young inspector smiled

confidently. "I'll swim beside you the whole way, until you reach shore. If you get in any trouble, I'll hold you up."

"Well...." He seemed so confident. Maybe she *could* do it, especially if he was there to catch her if she faltered.

Jean somehow summoned the energy to swim the entire distance. The safety inspector didn't say much, but true to his word, he matched his strokes to hers and watched her carefully. In a final burst of power, Jean stumbled trium- phantly onto the beach's sandy shore. Pat and the others, still lounging on their blankets, looked at her as she splashed through the shallows. "What happened to you?" Pat called. "You've been gone such a long time."

"I almost drowned," Jean panted, dragging herself to- ward them. "If it wasn't for the lifeguard...."

"What lifeguard?" Pat was looking past Jean.

"The guard, the safety inspector who swam back with me." Jean turned around to point to him.

But there was no young man on the shore, no one swim- ming away in the lake, no one walking on the shoreline in either direction. Nor had Jean's friends seen anyone accom- panying her.

Jean never saw her rescuer again, but she did discover that the resort didn't have any lifeguards or "safety inspec- tors" on the payroll. Perhaps he was a guard of a different kind.

# Angels on the Highway

*"See, I am sending an angel ahead of you to guard you along the way..."*

EXODUS 23:20

One of the first things I noticed as I opened my mail was that my son Tim had plenty of company—many people seemed to meet angels when driving! When you consider how much trouble we can get into in traffic, it's reasonable that our angels would be kept busy. For example, a minister's wife told me of a trip she took across central Kentucky. On one two-lane stretch she found herself stuck behind a coal truck, and after carefully peeking around, she swung out to pass. Horrified, she saw a huge semi coming toward her.

"The coal-truck driver saw my dilemma and inched over to the right as far as he could go, but there was not going to be enough space for three vehicles to pass, nor was there enough time for me to get back in my lane," she recounts. Frozen, she waited for the inevitable crash.

But as the truck approached her, it melted from view.

Shocked, she moved back behind the coal truck, checking her rearview mirror. The semi wasn't there. "There were five of us in the car," she told me. "All of us saw the truck coming. None of us saw what happened to it."

There were other stories as well:

* * *

Sharon W. (not her real name) doesn't drive often, so when she set out one rainy evening for a coworker's house, her roommate gave her explicit directions. But the rain turned to snow, and Sharon became nervous. She knew she didn't have enough experience driving in rough Michigan weather.

Traveling too fast through an intersection, Sharon tapped the brake, but her car skidded dangerously toward a light pole instead. "Oh, angels, help me!" she cried. Immediately the car righted itself.

"It was as if it had actually been picked up and turned around," she says. "I found myself on the right side of the street, heading in the right direction." None the worse for wear, Sharon drove on to her destination.

When she arrived home, Sharon told her roommate about the near miss. "I'm not surprised," her friend replied. "After you left, I began worrying about you driving in this weather. So I sent my guardian angel to accompany you."

Bernadine Jones was driving north on a two-way street in Denver, and approached an intersection where she could either continue on a straight path or go left into a curve. She was planning to turn left, but she was unfamiliar with the avenue, so when she heard a voice command her to "Slow down now!" she responded without thinking.

Coming almost to a stop, Bernadine was astonished to see an oncoming car speed across the left-hand curve, just where she would have been had she not stepped on the brake.

It was only later that Bernadine realized the voice had come from within her car. But she was alone.

* * *

Mae Warrick left the optometrist and walked toward her car. As she opened the front door, she heard a man's voice say, "Fasten that seat belt!" Mae turned and looked back, expecting to see someone, but the street was deserted.

Was someone playing a trick on her? Puzzled, she fastened the belt. She drove to her favorite highway café and started to turn left into the driveway. Too late, Mae realized that a truck was in the driveway and she couldn't complete her turn. A westbound car, unable to stop in time, plowed into Mae's automobile.

"Even with my seat belt on, I sustained a cracked rib and bruises," says this eighty-year-old. "I wonder what shape I would have been in, had I not obeyed my angel's orders!"

Janet Notte-Corrao obeyed orders too one night. She was sitting in the passenger seat next to her husband, their two children in the back. Janet was not really alarmed to hear a voice as the car went around a curve—she has heard her angel before. Although the message was not audible to the others, Janet heard: "Pray, Janet! There is a car coming that will hit you as you turn into your driveway. Pray!"

As she heard the words, Janet also received a vision of the vehicle hitting her family's car. *Oh, God,* she prayed, *please surround our car with Your heavenly host of angels!*

Janet's husband was driving carefully. Without warning, there was the sound of screeching tires, and then a jolt as he slammed on the brakes.

"I was still so deep in prayer that the motion was almost a surprise," Janet says. "It thrust me forward—thanks to my seat belt, *not* through the windshield—but the cars hadn't crashed. We were so close that their headlights were shining into our eyes."

Before Janet's astonished husband could react, the other car sped off, as quickly as it had appeared. But her prayer had been answered. "There was just a tiny space between the two cars," she notes with a smile. "A space the width of an angel."

Finally, driving home on a St. Louis freeway one rush hour, Andrew (not his real name) had almost reached his exit. Checking his mirrors, he turned the steering wheel to move into the right-hand lane. But the wheel didn't budge. What was happening? Andrew attempted to swerve again, but the wheel seemed stuck.

He would have to force it in order to get off the freeway and find a service station right away. Trying not to panic, Andrew looked back to see what was behind him.

Directly at his rear, in the blind spot, was a compact car. "It was too far back to be picked up by peripheral vision, too far forward to be seen in my rearview mirror. Had the steering not locked, I would have turned directly into the other vehicle, at fifty-five miles per hour."

Andrew braked a little, to let the other vehicle pass, before forcing his steering wheel to the right. But as soon as the little car went by, Andrew's wheel responded normally. There was no reason to find a service station after all.

Andrew drove the car another eighteen months, and his son and daughter-in-law are now driving it. No one has found any abnormalities in the steering, or anything else.

# A Pat on the Back from God

*The guardian angels of life sometimes fly so high as to be beyond our sight, but they are always looking down upon us.*

JEAN PAUL RICHTER

And one more story about driving.... It was in January 1948 when young Father Anthony Zimmerman arrived as a freshly minted Catholic missionary priest at Yokohama port in Japan. He was the first of his order, the Society of the Divine Word, to journey from America after World War II had ended, but he would eventually be joined by many more, along with priests being sent out of China before the Communists could catch up with them.

Father Anthony still remembers how he felt when his feet touched the pier after riding the waves for twelve days. "I felt myself swaying," he says, "and I watched as my 117 trunks of luggage were lined up for inspection." Inside were many articles for the war-deprived missionaries: army-surplus shoes, winter underwear, jackets, canned goods, even a bicycle and tiny motorcycle. General Douglas MacArthur had given the word that missionaries were welcome in Japan, and his command apparently cut the red tape—Japanese tax officials gave only a cursory inspection to the luggage and Father Anthony was waved on to start his new life in Japan.

"The missionaries in our Tokyo house gave me a warm welcome that night," Father Anthony recalls. "We went to chapel right away to thank God for the safe journey. I don't remember whether I thanked my guardian angel specifically, but I usually kept in touch with him at morning and evening prayers, so I probably nodded to him then too, asking that he accompany me during my future in Japan."

He went first to a mission in Tajimi, where he would study Japanese and teach English. Those were the days of food and fuel rationing, when Japanese families sold precious heirlooms at bargain prices to buy the necessities of life. As they saw Americans helping them, giving them food and fuel and kind treatment, the environment slowly changed to mutual acceptance and tolerance. Yet living conditions were not comfortable.

"Traveling took a long time, there was no flush plumbing and we didn't always like the food. When I once asked my superior what that terrible smell was, he answered, 'Either it's supper or the toilet,'" Father Anthony says, adding that he commuted on rocky and deserted roads by a little putt-putt motorcycle. "Looking back, I think my guardian angel did not approve of all the risks I took, but I prayed to him daily and tried to keep him on my good side just in case."

By 1950, Father Anthony had relocated to Ehocho parish in Nagoya, but he still commuted to various sites to teach English, visit the hospitalized and, if the Japanese people were willing, to discuss the Christian message of healing and forgiveness. On occasion he would make rounds at the Umemori sanitarium for terminally ill tuberculosis patients. It was in the spring of 1950, after a visit to that sanitarium, that something special happened.

"After visiting with patients at Umemori, I packed everything into the jeep and started the drive back to Ehocho parish," he recalls. "I was never good at finding roads, but I drove on anyway, expecting that somehow I would return safely. I was not particularly attentive, being lost in a reverie about the people I had just left."

He was thinking about how desolate they were. In war-ravaged Japan, funds for the care of terminally ill patients were limited. The wait before death was gloomy, bereft of joy and hope. But a few were grateful to be told of God's love. For them, Father Anthony mused, his spirit still heavy at the sight of all that suffering, for them he could help open the gates of heaven.

He was nearing a crossroad now, but he didn't realize it was there. It was a wooded area, trees and shrubs crowded to the road's edge, and he saw only the continuous path of the road straight ahead. There was no stop sign, and he barreled the jeep onward to get home.

But, still deep in thought, Father Anthony felt a powerful jolt. *Oh, no!* he thought. *I've hit something really huge!* The jeep, traveling swiftly forward, began to rock dangerously up and down, and from side to side. It was like sitting on top of an earthquake. *Was* it an earthquake? What was happening?

Afraid of braking too hard and turning over, Father Anthony came slowly to a stop. And just in time. No more than fifteen yards ahead, an enormous truck came roaring from a side road that was hidden by the foliage and tore through the place where he would have been.

"If we had collided, the truck would have totaled both the jeep and me," he says. "Spontaneously I looked to heaven to thank God. I relish the moment still."

But what had gone wrong with the jeep? As his heart quieted from the near miss, he realized that he must have hit something large or, at the very least, blown a tire—a typical occurrence on those roads. Shakily, he got out to look. But there was nothing to see. The jeep seemed perfect—its tires were fine and he saw no dents or scrapes. And the road was completely smooth, without a rock or obstruction anywhere.

Frowning, Father Anthony got in again and started the engine. Flawless. As he pulled away, the jeep ran smoothly, with no hint of the shaking that had just taken place.

There was nothing wrong with it, absolutely nothing. But something mighty had manhandled it and changed Father Anthony's course. It was then that he realized what had happened and spoke to his guardian angel. "Sorry about that," he said. "And thank you very much."

Later Father Anthony learned that he was not the only priest to have been similarly graced. During that same period, a classmate, Father John, went routinely to a convent near Peking to say mass for the sisters there. He knew the route very well—a simple straight path. One morning he called a native with a pedicab to take him by that direct route.

Peking was already surrounded by the Communists, and the rumble of distant artillery could be heard. "Straight ahead," Father John said to the man operating the pedicab.

"No, sir!" the man said.

Father John was used to bargaining, but this time it was different. The man had already started a roundabout route that would take fifteen minutes longer and cost more. "Straight ahead!" Father John again insisted.

"No!"

"You win." Father John sat back in defeat as the pedicab began its circuitous and seemingly senseless journey.

But the route had not been pointless. For as they traveled,

a massive explosion ripped through the air and a bomb made a direct hit on the straight road where Father John would have been. Who can say whether the pedicab operator was an angel—or simply inspired by one? But as both priests know, angels take special care of missionaries.

"What does it feel like at such a time?" Father Anthony asks. "It feels like a pat on the back from God, Who says, 'I know you're here, and I like what you're doing. I also have more work that I want you to do. So hang in there! But be more careful!' One does not forget such a time and event."

Father Anthony eventually earned a doctorate and taught in Japan. Now retired, he has a new career, writing books on theology. "I suspect that in heaven, my guardian angel is going to tell me that he already knew all this was coming for me, and that is one of the reasons he made the jeep rock to keep me from being killed," he says. "The episode is etched into my memory. It is a gift I will never forget."

# Angels on Guard

*And Elisha prayed, "O Lord, open his eyes so he may see." Then the Lord opened the servant's eyes, and he looked and saw the hills full of horses and chariots of fire all around Elisha.*

2 KINGS 6:17

*P*erhaps the most fascinating angelic intervention is that which occurs when *other* people see a figure and the protected one doesn't see anything at all. The Bible offers several examples. The one in the quotation above describes Elisha, God's prophet, seeing the angels clearly, but the servant seeing only the opposing army—until his spiritual eyes are opened.

You will read similar stories here. Author Betty Malz gave me the example of her friend Bill (who didn't want his real name revealed). Bill, his wife, and two children were vacationing at Big Bear Lake in California, near Apple Valley. His wife was cooking on the open fire, and Bill took several photos of the family gathered around the fire. Then he read the Bible, asking God to protect them and give them a safe vacation.

In a moment, however, their peaceful surroundings were shattered by six men on motorcycles, who seemed to roar out of nowhere. One pulled a gun, demanding that the stunned family put their billfolds and purses on the ground.

Terrified, they did so, and Bill, in his haste, dropped his camera too.

All of a sudden, as quickly as they came, the men seemed to be stricken with fright. Leaving the family's belongings on the ground, they turned, ran for their motorcycles, and sped off. Why had they gone so suddenly, leaving behind the items they intended to steal?

Confused but relieved, Bill's family gave thanks to God for sparing them a terrible ordeal, then went on to enjoy the rest of their vacation. It was not until they arrived home and had their photos developed that they saw what the bikers had apparently seen that night.

One of the photos clearly shows the form of a white-clad angel patiently standing watch over the family as they sat around the fire.

Louis Torres, a youth minister who now works in Mexico, was the director of a Teen Challenge Center in Philadelphia. He spoke to Betty's church congregation one morning and further confirmed the Biblical perception of angels as strong soldiers who sometimes remain invisible except to those who need to see them in order to be convinced. In *Angels Watching Over Me*, Betty reports this story about a young woman named Myra, which Torres told her congregation:

Myra worked for Teen Challenge at the time Torres did. Since it was located in a rough part of the inner city, she was concerned for the teens who had shown interest in receiving Christian counsel. It was difficult for them to visit the center because on the streets just outside, a group from one of the local gangs repeatedly harassed them. For a short while each evening, Myra was alone at the Center, and the gang both-

ered her as well, banging on the door and shouting obsceni-
ties.

One night when the gang appeared, Myra suddenly felt
inspired to tell them about Jesus. Knowing the danger, she
first prayed for guidance. Yes, she felt sure she had heard the
Lord correctly. She opened the door and walked outside.

The gang moved around her and, keeping her voice
steady, she spoke to them about Jesus.

Instead of listening to her, however, the gang shouted
threats of drowning her in the nearby river. Trying to appear
calm, Myra walked back through the door of the Center and
shut it. They didn't follow her.

The next evening the thugs were back, once again banging on the door and threatening her life. Still believing she
should try and reach out to them, Myra breathed a prayer to
Jesus. "Lord, let your angels come with me and protect me,"
she murmured.

Then she opened the door and was about to speak when
the gang members suddenly stopped their shouting, turned
to look at one another and left silently and quickly. Myra was
surprised. Why had they gone?

The gang did not return for several days. Then one afternoon, to the surprise of everyone, they entered the Center in
an orderly fashion. Much later, after a relationship of trust
had been built with them, Louis Torres asked them what had
made them drop their threats against Myra and leave so
peacefully that night.

One young man spoke up. "We wouldn't dare touch her
after her boyfriend showed up. That dude had to be seven
feet tall."

"I didn't know Myra had a boyfriend," replied Louis

thoughtfully. "But at any rate, she was alone here that night."

"No, we saw him," insisted another gang member. "He was right behind her.

"He was big as life in his classy white suit." [8]

# Special Delivery

*"...For God will deign*
*To visit oft the dwellings of just men*
*Delighted, and with frequent intercourse*
*Thither will send his winged messengers*
*On errands of supernal grace."*

MILTON, *PARADISE LOST*

$\mathcal{I}$ first heard of Kenneth Ware through Betty Malz, who profiled him in *Angels Watching Over Me*. The Assemblies of God headquarters in Springfield, Missouri, provided more information:

Kenneth Ware was born in Tennessee. A short time later, his father was killed in World War I, and his mother took Kenneth back to Switzerland, where she had grown up.

At seventeen, Kenneth became an Assemblies of God minister, going first to Jerusalem, and later to the south of France, where he met and married the sixteen-year-old daughter of Max Vinitski, an orthodox Jew turned Christian and an artist whose portraits hang in the Louvre. Kenneth became known in Paris as a great evangelist, and when World War II broke out, both the Vinitski and Ware homes became havens for Jewish fugitives fleeing to Spain or Switzerland.

As a son of an American soldier, husband of a Jew, and supporter of the French resistance, Kenneth was in constant danger of being imprisoned. Eventually Kenneth, Suzie, and their infant son tried to flee France. Instead, Kenneth was arrested, interrogated, and beaten, but when a German guard discovered he was a pastor, he was secretly released.

Finally reunited with his wife and son in Lausanne, Switzerland, Kenneth tried to provide for them. One Saturday morning in September 1944, however, he found himself without a penny. Suzie decided to pray—specifically. "God, I need five pounds of potatoes, two pounds of pastry flour, apples, pears, a cauliflower, carrots, veal cutlets for Saturday, and beef for Sunday," she said.

A few hours later, someone knocked on the door. Suzie opened it to a man carrying a basket of groceries. The man, between thirty and forty years old, was over six feet tall and strong looking, with blue eyes, white-blond hair, and a long blue apron over his work clothes. He seemed radiant, glowing. "Mrs. Ware," he said, "I'm bringing you what you asked for." He spoke in perfect French, without the usual Swiss accent.

"There must be some mistake," Suzie protested, bewildered. "I have not ordered anything." She called Kenneth.

Kenneth did not think the man looked like an ordinary deliveryman. Perhaps he was the owner of a firm and had gotten the apartment numbers mixed up. "There are twenty-five apartments here, sir. Have you come to the wrong one?" he asked.

The man ignored the question. "Mrs. Ware," he repeated, "I am bringing what you asked for." Then he went into the kitchen and emptied the basket. On the table were the exact items Suzie had requested from God that morning—even the two pounds of pastry flour was the correct brand. The Wares were shocked. "I turned to apologize, to explain that I hadn't a coin to give him, but his look of reproach sealed my lips," Kenneth reported.

Suzie accompanied the man to the door and thanked him, then the couple stood by the window to watch him leave the building—via the only route available. But though Kenneth watched, and Suzie opened the door again to check the hallway, the man never went by.

After the war, the Wares returned to a Paris crowded with refugees. They set up missions and schools, and were able to feed, clothe, comfort, and educate the destitute. Eventually, they retired to the south of France.

Kenneth Ware always maintained he would recognize the deliveryman anywhere if he saw him again. He never did. But Kenneth and Suzie were filled with gratitude to the God Who would send a personal shopper to fill their needs.

# Message from Beyond

*But all God's angels come to us disguised...*
JAMES RUSSELL LOWELL
*"ON THE DEATH OF A FRIEND'S CHILD"*

Sister Mary Dolores Kazmierczak was planning the trip of a lifetime—Rome, then on to Poland. Her elderly father wanted to accompany her, but Sister Mary Dolores was unwilling to extend the invitation. "First, my mother wouldn't fly, and since one of them never went anywhere without the other, I didn't think Dad would be happy on a trip without her," she explains.

The second reason was more awkward. Mr. Kazmierczak had a physical disorder that caused him to lose his equilibrium. This shakiness would come on without warning. How, Sister Mary Dolores wondered, would she manage him on an extensive trip? What if he fell and hurt himself? Her decision was logical, she knew, but she still felt guilty.

However, two months before the trip, in May of 1979, Mrs. Kazmierczak died. Now Sister Mary Dolores's father was terribly lonely and her guilt feelings worsened. He would so enjoy traveling. But her reluctant answer was still no. Taking him anywhere would be too risky.

A few days before she was to leave for Europe, Sister Mary Dolores and her father visited Mrs. Kazmierczak's grave at Holy Cross Cemetery in Calumet City, Illinois. On their way home they passed a small roadside produce stand. It looked deserted, but Mr. Kazmierczak wanted some fruit, so they pulled in to see if anyone was there.

Two men were running the stand. One, wearing a blue shirt, was behind the counter; the other, in brown pants and a hat, was arranging the tables. Sister Mary Dolores and her father were the only customers there, and none of the four exchanged any comments or greetings.

Mr. Kazmierczak wandered around looking at the displays while Sister Mary Dolores, keeping him in view as always lest he lose his balance, selected some produce. She gave her money to the blue-shirted worker at the cash register, then started toward her father, just a few feet away. It was then that the man in the hat approached her. "It's okay to take your dad on the trip," he told her without any preamble.

"What trip?" What was he talking about?

"The trip you're going on," the man replied. "I just spoke with your mother, and she said it was okay to take your dad. Nothing bad will happen to him."

"How could you have spoken to my mother?" Sister Mary Dolores demanded. "She died this past May."

"Yes, I know," he said.

Sister Mary Dolores looked around in astonishment. She and her father were still the only customers in view. Had her father complained to the man that he was being left behind? Yet the lot was so small—surely she would have seen or overheard a conversation. She could confront her father in front of the stranger, but Dad might be embarrassed or upset. It was better to wait until they were alone.

"Well...thank you," she said to the man, who was still

standing calmly in front of her, and then she hurried her father to the car.

Once they were on the highway, she broached the subject. "Dad, what did you say to the man at the fruit stand?"

"I didn't talk to him," Mr. Kazmierczak said. "You paid him."

"I'm not talking about the man at the cash register, Dad. It was the other one, in the hat."

"But. . . ." Her father's face was troubled. "I didn't see a second person. There was only the one man in the blue shirt, behind the counter."

"You saw me talking to the second man. You must have— you were right there the whole time, just a few feet away."

"But I didn't. There wasn't anyone else there."

Sister Mary Dolores stopped talking. She didn't want to upset her father. And slowly she was realizing that something supernatural had just taken place.

During subsequent summers Sister Mary Dolores took her father with her on airplane and auto trips to Arizona and all through the state of Michigan. He never had a fall, thrived on the change of scene, and died a fulfilled man at ninety-two.

"I never worried after the incident at the fruit stand," Sister Mary Dolores says. She knew her mother was looking out for both of them, and had sent an angel to tell them so.

# The Man in White

*How did he get thar? Angels.*
*He could never have walked in that storm.*
*They jest scooped down and toted him*
*To whar it was safe and warm...*
    JOHN HAY, *"LITTLE BREECHES"*

Three years ago the Durrance family, natives of southwestern Florida, moved to a house in a partially completed subdivision, once farmland. Set apart by side roads, the Durrance house was the only dwelling on their street, and their vast lot was surrounded by woodsy grass, palmetto clumps, and drainage ditches.

Even without a telephone, Debbie Durrance felt comfortable in the isolated brushland, but she was apprehensive about letting her children roam at will. Things could happen—kids could get hurt in places where their cries couldn't be heard. And there had been several reports of rattlesnakes in the area; their pets had even been bitten. "Noise and traffic scare rattlers," Debbie explains, "but they're very much at home in a quiet area like ours."

Still, one lazy Sunday afternoon just before Easter, when twelve-year-old Mark decided to wander the land with his BB gun and his dog, Debbie agreed. She started the dinner dishes, enjoying the peace and quiet of the mild day.

Mark was enjoying the sunshine too. Spying a bird in a

clump of palm, he leaped over a drainage ditch for a closer view, landed on something movable—and felt a burst of agony as if his foot had exploded. In horror, he realized that a huge rattlesnake was hanging on to his foot, puncturing his shoe right below the ankle. Mark had never felt pain this intense. And the snake's fangs seemed to be stuck in his ankle! Through a haze, Mark saw his dog growling and snapping at the snake, which eventually released its grip and slithered away.

But the rattler's deadly venom had entered at the main vein in Mark's leg, the worst place for a bite. By now, that vein was carrying poison through Mark's body, attacking every system. Horrified, Mark realized that his strength was ebbing quickly, and he could barely walk. That 150 yards home might as well be 150 miles. He was going to die out here—and his family didn't even know he was hurt.

Debbie was putting away the dishes when she heard the front door open and her older son shout, "Mark, what's wrong?"

In horror, she heard Mark answer, "I've been rattlesnake-bit." She raced to the living room, just as Mark fell to the floor. Pulling off his shoe as Buddy ran for his father, Debbie saw the foot already swollen and purple, and she smelled the same musky odor that she had noticed when her pets had been bitten. It was true—a snake *had* bitten him. And it was not a simple flesh wound. Debbie began to tremble. Without a phone, they would have to drive Mark seventeen miles to the nearest emergency center. Would there be time? *Not my child, God,* she prayed. *Please, not Mark!*

Her husband, Bobby, raced in and picked up his son. The family ran to their truck and sped down the highway. Mark was already having convulsions, and his breathing grew fainter. The only thing Debbie could do in the tense and silent truck cab was pray.

As they neared the emergency center, however, steam floated from the truck's hood. It was overheating! "Bobby, what are we going to do if it stops?" Debbie asked in panic, but it was already too late. Bobby braked for another car and the engine died. The Durrances were in the middle of traffic, but although Bobby leaped from the cab and tried to flag someone down, vehicles just kept going around them.

Then an old compact car pulled over. The driver was a Haitian farmworker who didn't speak English, but the family's frantic actions told him all he needed to know. Debbie and Buddy dragged Mark into the car. "The driver sped off, following my pointing and wild gestures, and we arrived at the emergency center just a short time later," Debbie says.

At the center, a team attempted to stabilize Mark. "Usually a snakebite could be treated at an emergency center," Debbie explains. "But because the venom in Mark's leg had hit a main vein, he was being poisoned at a more rapid rate and needed special care." By the time an ambulance had been summoned to take him to the nearest hospital in Naples, ten miles away, Mark had lapsed into a coma.

For the next twelve hours the Naples hospital staff worked on Mark. Debbie and Bobby sensed that the team didn't think their son would survive. Debbie continued to pray.

During the next few days, every part of Mark's body stopped functioning except his heart. The venom bloated him, swelling his eyes so tightly closed that his lashes were barely visible. His kidneys failed. A respirator moved his lifeless lungs up and down. Internal hemorrhaging caused blood to seep not only from his ears, mouth, and eyes but also from his pores; he required transfusions of eighteen pints of blood before the nightmare had ended. There was a ninety percent chance he would lose his leg, and it swelled so large that eventually the doctors slashed it from top to bottom to relieve the pressure. Every new symptom was worse than the last.

Debbie sat for hours by his bedside, praying aloud and talking to her son. "I hoped Mark might hear my words to him and to God," she says. "I wanted him to know that I believed he would live."

Miraculously, Mark began to improve. Gradually he emerged from the coma and began writing to his parents on a tablet. Then one day the doctors took him off the respirator. And though his voice was scratchy, Mark began to tell them of his terrible ordeal.

"It was a rattler. It stuck on my shoe and wouldn't let go...."

"But where were you?" Mark's father wanted to know.

"Out in the fields, next to the ditch."

"But that's at least 150 yards!"

"He must have been much closer," one of the doctors said, shaking his head. "Mark could never have walked that far. There was too much venom in his system—he would have been unconscious right away."

And there were the thirteen steps up the front of the house to the living room. How had this terribly wounded boy managed to climb them?

"The man in white helped me," Mark explained, in answer to their questions.

"Man? What man?" Debbie asked.

"The man. He was just ... there. When I knew I couldn't make it to the house, he picked me up and carried me."

"What did he look like?" Debbie felt a tingle on the back of her neck.

"I never saw his face, only from his shoulders down. But he had on a white robe and his arms were real strong. He reached down and picked me up, and I was hurting so bad that I just sort of leaned my head on him. I felt calm."

"Did he say anything, Mark?"

"He talked to me in a deep voice," Mark answered. "He told me I was going to be real sick, but not to worry. Then he carried me up the stairs and I didn't see him again."

A man in white.... Debbie didn't know what to say. Had her son dreamed the whole thing? But how had he gotten home?

Mark was in the hospital for nine weeks. Later he had numerous grafts to rebuild the muscle and tissue at the back of his leg. But doctors expect him to suffer no permanent damage.

"While Mark was recovering, he told me that he was sure his Grand-Daddy Durrance had been with him in the hospital emergency room," Debbie says. "There's an old custom in Georgia that if you walk a newborn baby around the house three times, the baby will be like you. Grand-Daddy Durrance had done that with Mark, and the two had always been close."

But Mark's grandfather had died some time before the accident, and Debbie reminded Mark of this. "But he was right there with me, Mom," Mark insisted. "I know he was."

Of course! Grand-Daddy Durrance must have been the man in white that Mark dreamed of seeing.

But Mark was firm. "No, Mom, that wasn't Grand-Daddy. And I didn't *dream* about the man in white. He was real."

Mark's experience has touched many people. The Durrances had a thankyou note to the Haitian farmer published in the newspaper. They never found him, but their note inspired readers to think about their own responses to people in trouble. Debbie is a hairdresser, and because the family received so much publicity at the time, customers occasionally recognize her and she is able to tell them of her belief that God does indeed answer prayer. She also visits other snakebite victims to comfort and encourage them.

Today her son leads a normal teenage life. Except for one difference—the awareness that something very special happened to him out in that Florida brushland. Mark Durrance passed through the valley of death as few people ever do—and had an unforgettable Easter awakening.

# Stranger on the Road

*...And I think that saving a little child,*
*And fotching him to his own,*
*Is a derned sight better business*
*Than loafing around the Throne.*
        JOHN HAY, *"LITTLE BREECHES"*

$\mathcal{E}$dward Strnad has had a long and affectionate relationship with angels. The youngest of eleven children—and the only one with dimples—he once asked his mother where he got them.

"That's where the angels kissed you!" she laughed.

But the Strnad family also lived through the Great Depression and knew firsthand how it felt to be hungry. When Edward grew up and raised his own family, he often volunteered for various food-collection banks, determined to do whatever he could to help the less fortunate. Thus, it was natural that he would notice the child...and take action.

Edward drives into Cleveland every morning on I–77. At East 30th Street, he says, there is an on ramp and three lanes that split to form I–90. One overcast and blustery winter morning, he spotted a young boy leaning into the wind, walking on the right shoulder of the hazardous highway. Although clean and neat, he was dressed too lightly for Cleveland's raw weather, wearing only a short poplin jacket and no hat or gloves. Under his arm were a few books.

Edward was astonished. "My first thought was that the boy should not be there at all—it was far too dangerous," he says. "But by this time I had passed him." Edward could not bring himself to abandon the child. Somehow he was able to cross three lanes of rush-hour traffic before the interstate split and pull onto the berm. He could see the boy behind him, and as the child approached, Edward rolled down the electric window. "Where are you going?" he asked. "And why are you walking along this open highway?"

"The bus forgot to pick me up," the child explained. He looked about nine or ten. "I'm going to school."

"What school?"

"Tremont, on Tenth Street."

Edward frowned. Tremont was on Cleveland's near west side, quite a distance. Why would this child be going there?

Then Edward realized that the boy was probably part of Cleveland's integration-busing program and would indeed attend class far from home. To reach Tremont this morning on foot, however, he still had to negotiate three lanes of high-speed traffic, cross a windy bridge and another heavily traveled avenue—at least a three-mile trip. "Would you like a ride to school?" Edward asked.

The boy shook his head, but stayed where he was. The warm car was obviously tempting.

"You're right not to accept rides from strangers," Edward reassured him, taking identification out of his wallet. "But see? My son is a police officer, and I have an honorary badge with my son's number, marked 'Father.' And here's my driver's license...." The boy studied the photos carefully, apparently torn between wanting a ride and worrying about his safety. "I understood his fear. I'd told my own children never to accept a ride from a stranger," Edward says. But he had to wait until the child made up his mind. Eventually the freezing wind won and the child hesitantly got into the car.

Edward stayed as quiet and nonthreatening as possible, just keeping his eyes on the road. "We didn't exchange more than ten words on the way," he says, "only those necessary for directions." It was important that this little boy feel safe. His journey today had been difficult enough already.

At last they arrived at Tremont school, an old brick building in one of Cleveland's poorest but quaintly charming sections (now called Ohio City). There was a tubular fence about two feet tall around the front lawn, but not a person in sight—no traffic, no noise, not even a patrol boy walking across the playground. "It almost looked like school was closed," Edward recalls. "But of course the weather was nasty, and classes would have already started."

Edward stopped, and without looking back, the child got out and started quickly up the walk to the school's front door. Before he had entered the building, Edward was already on his way.

Throughout the morning, however, Edward's thoughts returned to the little traveler. Odd that he happened to be on the highway, stranger still that Edward was able to shoot across three lanes of traffic without mishap to reach him. And it bothered Edward that he had not actually *watched* the child safely enter the building.... Finally, he phoned the school just to make sure his little passenger, although late, was safely in class.

But Edward was in for a surprise. School was indeed in session, but the woman who answered the phone reassured Edward that no child had been tardy that morning.

"But I dropped him off right in front of the building, after school had started," Edward protested.

"No one can enter the building after the bell rings, sir," the woman explained. "Everything is locked as soon as the children are checked in. He would have had to be admitted by an adult. And no child was late today."

Edward sighed. "Then he must have played hookey. Or ...what if something happened to him?"

"I can inquire," she said. "Can you describe him?"

Edward did, and then waited while the woman did some checking. When she came back, she seemed as puzzled as he. "No child answers your description," she told him. "And attendance records don't show *any* child missing today. Every youngster who's supposed to be here is accounted for."

To this day, some seven years later, the episode is still vivid, Edward says. But it's harder for him to understand the *why* of it all. Perhaps Edward was used or "tested" in a way he still does not fully understand. Maybe the incident affects others in its retelling.

Whatever the reason, Edward is confident that he will one day meet the child again. "He was brown," Edward told me. "I am white. What color are angels?"

# Scaling the Heights

*But if these beings guard you, they do so because*
*they have been summoned by your prayers.*

SAINT AMBROSE

$\mathcal{C}$an angels rescue us even when we never see them? Even from something as commonplace as weather?

On a very stormy and blustery morning, seventy-nine-year-old Anna May Arthur was climbing the steep steps of a cathedral in her native Ireland. She knew she should have used the front staircase, which provides a railing and some shelter, but she had cut through the churchyard, and the back flight was handier.

As she climbed, the wind buffeted her and she felt unsteady and vulnerable. Since most churchgoers enter from the front, there wasn't a soul around to help her stay upright, no one on whom to lean. "I envisioned losing my balance, falling backward, and cracking my poor head open," Anna May relates. "I wondered if anyone would even find me."

The forty steps were starting to feel like four hundred. As the frail woman approached the top, her fears came to pass—an especially strong gust caught her and she started to tumble backward.

Instinctively Anna May appealed to heaven, crying, "Oh,

my guardian angel, save me!" Immediately she felt two strong hands on her back, pushing her forward and erect.

"I really wasn't surprised," Anna May says. "In fact, it crossed my mind that when I turned, I would actually see a heavenly being in white! What did one say to one's angel, I wondered."

But when Anna May turned, she saw a neighbor holding her upright. She had known Thomas Hillen for years, and was aware that he suffered with very bad heart trouble. Because of his debilitating illness, Thomas always walked at a snail's pace. Had he risked his own health to save her?

"As I came in the yard, I saw you sway and start to go backward down the steps," Thomas told Anna May.

"But, Thomas, how did you get up here so fast?"

"That's just it! I don't know!" His face was bewildered. He had been at the church gate, at least forty paces from the bottom step, when he saw Anna May lose her balance at the top of the flight.

And suddenly *he* was there too, across the courtyard and up the steps, right behind her. "I don't remember crossing the distance. I—I seem to have been carried," Thomas told her. "And yet, that would be humanly impossible."

Shocked, Anna May looked at him more closely. He was not even winded. How could a heart patient—or even a long-distance runner—have covered that span during the split second when Anna May began to fall and called to her angel?

She looked around, but there was still no one within sight, no one who might have helped in some way. She and Thomas had been the only ones in the churchyard.

Confounded, the two discussed the event for a while, looking for logical explanations, then went into church to give thanks. "I had always been aware of my guardian angel, in a vague kind of way, but nothing as positive and dramatic as this has ever happened to me, before or since," Anna May says. "But then, there are always those little 'accidents' where one feels one is fortunate to have escaped injury. Is such a thing always a coincidence?"

Anna May leaves the answer to others.

Diane Barnard (not her real name) doesn't believe in coincidences, either. She remembers a very special Christmas Eve when she asked for help—and received it.

Snow had been falling all that day in Rittman, Ohio. The white covering was now almost a foot deep, and although it looked beautiful, driving was virtually impossible. For twenty-three-year-old Diane, however, walking was just fine. Even though she lived more than a mile from church, she was so happy to be going to midnight services that she didn't mind the trek—or the fact that she would have to travel alone because her husband would stay home and care for their toddler. Christmas was just the very best time of year!

At about eleven P.M. Diane said good-bye to her husband and set out. Although the drifts were quite high in places, the journey was downhill, and she got to the church with time to spare.

The festive and beautiful ceremony ended just before one A.M. Diane hadn't encountered neighbors or friends who might have given her a ride home, so she started her hike. But getting *up* the hill was a far different matter from going down. Each step now seemed deeper and more difficult than the one preceding it, and her path was both dark and deserted, with no homes nearby. Diane's breathing came in small gasps as she plodded onward. Oh, she was tired! And as she passed a barren wooded area, she became even more alarmed.

"My feet were getting heavier with each step, and I started to realize that I was in trouble," she says. "There was a distinct possibility that I actually wasn't going to make it home—I was just too cold and weary. Would my husband wake up and realize I was missing? Would anyone find me here, or would I fall and freeze?" Her joyous excursion was rapidly turning into a nightmare.

Diane looked at her watch: one-fifteen. There was still a long way to go to reach warmth and safety, and her strength was virtually at an end. She gazed at the star-studded Christmas heavens. "Oh, God, I'm so afraid," she blurted. "Help me to get home!"

Suddenly Diane heard beautiful music—and felt herself floating on top of the snow, as if she were in a dream. What was happening? Was she freezing? Is this how it felt to die?

No. She was, oddly, in front of her house. But how could this be? Diane blinked, looked at the familiar landmarks, then at her watch again. It was one-twenty. And yet she had no memory of moving since she had prayed. Certainly five minutes had not elapsed. Nor would she, in her exhausted condition, have been able to scale the steep hill looming in front of her. She had been ready to lie down in the snow and give up the struggle.

And yet she was safely home and feeling...exultant.

The young mother entered her quiet house and, still wearing her coat and boots, sat in a chair and looked at the winking Christmas lights. "I don't remember how long I sat," she says now, "but I knew something strange had happened to me, and I was afraid even to admit it to myself.

"But I've come up with no other explanation in all the

years since then. I think it was an angel, commanded by God to carry me safely to my front door." A member of the heavenly host, perhaps, leaving his duties on a Bethlehem hillside to touch a young woman in Ohio.

These women both *asked* for help in dangerous situations, tapping into an invisible source of strength and grace. "Perhaps angels won't intervene unless we ask them," one respondent summed it up. "But we should—most of us need all the help we can get!"

# The Flutter of Wings

*Writ in the climate of heaven, in the language spoken
by angels.*

LONGFELLOW
*"THE CHILDREN OF THE LORD'S SUPPER"*

In the early 1960s, Lee Ballard, a missionary linguist, was
sent by the Summer Institute of Linguistics to a remote village in the Philippine Islands. His job was to lay groundwork
for the eventual task of transcribing Ibaoli, a completely ver-
bal language, into written form.

It's difficult to imagine societies that can't write their
words. We take our inscribed languages so for granted that
we forget that, for some cultures, sound is still the only
means of communication.

And that's the talent of linguists—to reframe those sounds
into something readable. They do this first by immersing
themselves in the spoken words. Gradually they describe a
sound system, analyze its grammar, begin a dictionary, collect folklore, tape dialogue—all aimed at ultimately inscrib-
ing speech. Lee Ballard's group had a second agenda as well:
After developing text, they hoped to write a Bible in Ibaoli
for the villagers.

The institute had selected this particular village because
no one there spoke English and Ballard could immerse himself in the language. On the night of this incident, he had

been there five months. Ballard told his story originally in the May 1986 issue of *Dallas* magazine:

He told me his name was Pug-Pug. And of course I believed him. More than a year was to pass before I learned that "pug-pug" in his language meant "amputated." Maybe he told me Pug-Pug was his name because he knew it would be easy for me to remember. He wanted me to tell my neighbors his name and have them laugh and tell me no one was named Amputated and shrug it off as a joke. He knew it would make me think.

You see, as I look back on the incident and weigh the alternatives, I think Pug-Pug was an angel.

Pug-Pug came to visit on a night of chilled splendor. From my bench on the front porch I could see far off down the valley, past the tall banana trees and dull thatch of the village houses to the mountainside rising from the river with its sheer rocks glistening white in the moonlight. Only an occasional baby's cry or the bark of a dog broke the absolute still of midnight.

But I was not sitting there to absorb the view. My thoughts played and replayed the disheartening hours of my supervisor's visit just completed. He had come to the Philippines to measure my progress in learning the local language—and I had not even understood when a villager said my supervisor needed a haircut! I knew so many hundreds, even thousands, of words and phrases, and yet I was unable to handle conversation. I was deeply discouraged.

That is when Pug-Pug appeared. His boots clacked on the wooden ladder leading up to my porch, and I heard him say in deep raspy tones, *"Iyayak ali* (I am here)," the local equivalent of "Hi."

As I look back, several things were strange about his arrival. For one, tribal people rarely go out at night and never without a pitch pine torch. Even the most sophisticated fear the *ampasit* spirits that are said to live in rocks and trees. More remarkable was the fact that no dogs warned of his arrival.

In the surprise of that moment, I was only aware that his appearance and manner were different. He was forward and assertive in a place where shyness is a strong cultural value. And he wore boots and a heavy wool overcoat in a barefoot society where people wrap themselves in blankets.

I followed local etiquette and tried to make small talk. "Where have you come from?" I asked.

In return, he spoke directly. He told me immediately his name, that he had come from Baguio, where he worked for Benguet Consolidated Mining Company as an *osokiro*, a "tunneler." He volunteered his relationships in the village and his mission. He was looking, he said, for treasure—the millions in gold reportedly taken from the Philippine treasury by the fleeing Japanese in 1945. He thought it may have been stashed in a cave between our village and the town on the other side of the mountain.

We talked for an hour or more. I had read accounts of the war in our area, but he told me much more than I knew. And ...the entire conversation was in the tribal language—and I understood!

As we talked, I waited for this stranger to tell me why he had come to my house. But he never did. At one point in the conversation he stood up and said, "*Ondawakda* (I am going now)." He stepped quickly down the ladder, passed under the elevated porch and disappeared into the coffee grove.

In the morning I joined four or five men as they sat on a

wall next door, warming themselves in the day's early sunshine. I told them about my night visitor. When I came to
his name, they smiled. Then, one by one, their faces creased
and cracked into knee-slapping laughter.

"What did he look like?" asked one, wiping a tear from
his eye. He wanted to know who had played such a wonderful trick on me.

"He was big," I said, "with a long thick coat and boots.
He said he was Aloto's brother. He said he works in the
mines."

"Does Aloto have a brother in the mines?" one man asked
the others. "Or even a second or third cousin?"

"*Aychi met* (Emphatically not)," they all said. I heard one
of the men whisper to another, "Who probably was it?"

Who was it indeed? I have no idea. But I do not think his
mission in our valley was to hunt treasure. I think he came
because I was discouraged. And if I am right, he was suc-
cessful. For his visit that night marked a turning point in my
career. The success of that night's conversation gave me the
confidence I needed to succeed. Discouragement vanished
into the night with Pug-Pug.

Have you ever been visited by Pug-Pug, in one of his many
guises? Maybe not.

But then ... how do you know? [9]

"Had I been there only for business reasons, I doubt Pug-Pug
would have come to comfort me," says Ballard, now living
and working in the Dallas area. "But our organization had a
special motive, and perhaps that was why my work was
graced in such a unique way." By the mid-70s, both the New
Testament and a series of hymnals had been written in the
Ibaoli language. And when Ballard later returned to the area

as a tourist, a villager referred to him as "the man who gave us books."

Pug-Pug provided something far more valuable than gold to the villagers—and to one gifted linguist.

# Brian's Angel

*Angel of God, my guardian dear*
*To whom God's love commits me here;*
*Ever this day be at my side,*
*To light and guard, to rule and guide.*

TRADITIONAL CATHOLIC PRAYER

Zena Marie Anagnostou is the youngest in a family of seven, living in Antioch, California. She was a high school sophomore when her married sister, Rene, had her first baby, Brian. "My mom and I took care of him when Rene went back to work," Zena explains. "His bed was in my room, and he occasionally stayed overnight. We got to be very close."

Everyone who knew him agrees that Brian was the all-American boy. He had a zest for life and seemed to like everyone. As he grew, he became a class leader and a straight-A student.

Although the entire family is close, with cousins, aunts, and uncles all keeping up with one another's news, Zena and Brian had a special bond. "I took him and his younger brother, Sean, everywhere, to church, movies, walks around the lake," Zena remembers. "The boys came to visit me at college. We collected cans to recycle for their savings accounts. We talked about everything, all our dreams and thoughts."

One day when Brian was eleven, Zena was working the evening shift at the medical-records office at Roseville Hospital. Her sister Theresa came to break the news. "Zena, there's been an accident. It's Brian...."

"Brian! What happened?"

"He got hit by a bus on his way home from school." Theresa started to cry.

Zena stood in shock. It couldn't be happening. Was he a patient here? She'd have to go up to his room right away. "Theresa, where is he? Is he here, in Emergency? How bad is it?"

"He didn't make it. Zena, he's dead."

Zena refused to believe it. Even as they drove to the morgue, she couldn't comprehend such a loss. But slowly she was forced to accept the unthinkable. Brian had gotten off his school bus, heard the city bus coming up behind, and waited by the side of the road for it to pass. The city bus had cut back in front of the parked school bus, catching Brian and dragging him to his death.

Brian's death devastated the family. Zena seemed to walk in a fog. God would get her through it eventually, she knew, but right now the pain seemed unbearable.

Because Zena worked the evening shift at the hospital, she often came home at two or three A.M. One Sunday shortly after Brian's death, although she usually accompanied her family to the eight A.M. mass, Zena left word that she would sleep late and attend noon services by herself.

The church was sparsely occupied when Zena arrived, and it was very hot. She usually sits in front, so she went to the second pew, which had only one occupant, a boy about twelve. Even before Zena reached the pew, the youngster had gotten to his feet and stepped out into the aisle to let her in.

Zena slumped dispiritedly in the center of the pew. Some elderly ladies were sitting right behind them.

As the mass progressed, Zena noticed that the young boy was reciting the prayers perfectly. Not only was he saying the people's responses, he was also murmuring the priest's part, words that usually do not appear in the prayer book. "He just glowed with peace, and he was so pleasant to look at. He sang all the songs in a beautiful voice, without using the songbook," Zena says. Her sorrowing spirit began to lift. "I wanted to tell him how pleased I was to see a young person so tuned in to mass." She decided she would compliment him when services were over.

In many Catholic churches people hold hands while reciting the Lord's Prayer, and when that time arrived, the boy came smiling to Zena and took her hand. His hand was very warm and comfortable in hers. Zena felt a serenity seeping into her, like a balm soothing her raw emotions.

Holy Communion followed, and the people arose, pew by pew. Zena exited her pew and the boy stepped back so she could precede him to the altar. She received communion, stepped aside for a moment, "and out of the corner of my eye, I saw the boy receive communion next," she says. She began walking back to her pew, but glanced behind her, just to keep him in view.

But the boy was no longer there. In fact, although Zena had a clear view of all three nearby exits—and he couldn't have reached any in the few seconds that had elapsed—he had simply disappeared. Quickly she scanned the aisles, but there was no sign of him anywhere.

At the end of mass, Zena was still thinking about the boy. Odd that someone so obviously reverent would leave mass before it ended. Had the heat made him ill? She followed the elderly ladies down the aisle and out into the sunshine. "You didn't happen to notice where that boy went," she asked them, "the one who sat in front of you during mass?"

The ladies looked at each other, then, puzzled, at Zena. "There was no boy in front of us, dear," one told her gently. "You were alone in the pew."

Brian's family has been comforted ever since. Surely his guardian angel sent Zena a signal that all is well.

# Unseen Protectors

*A shiver runs down your spine when you realize it is not our imagination. Something is watching us out there.*

SOPHY BURNHAM, *A BOOK OF ANGELS*

How many times are we kept from danger by an unseen guardian? Some people are fortunate enough to know. In 1960, the well-known Dr. Norman Vincent Peale preached a sermon that included a story about an Episcopal minister in a Southern town who stood up to Sam, a political boss, and was able to defeat a plan of his. "I'm going to kill that minister," Sam told several of his friends after the meeting.

Friends alerted the minister and offered to walk home with him, past a dark woods. But the minister waved away their concerns. "The Lord will be with me," he told them, and he walked home alone in safety.

Years passed, and on his deathbed, Sam sent for this minister. "Reverend, I meant to kill you that night," he said. "I was in the woods with a club."

"Why didn't you?" the minister asked.

"What do you mean—why didn't I?" Sam asked. "Who were those two big men with you?"

"There were no big men with me," the minister protested.

"Yes, there were," Sam said. "I saw them."

* * *

Several writers told of similar events. Suzanne Vecchiarelli of New City, New York, was visiting a friend in the hospital and had brought her a copy of a book about angels. When the friend's roommate saw the book, she became very emotional and told the women a story about her cousin Stacey (not her real name).

Stacey, then in her mid-twenties, lived in a poorer section of Brooklyn, New York, an area with many tenements. One night while Stacey was walking home from work, she saw a man ahead of her, loitering against a building. Stacey had an immediate feeling of fear; there had been some recent muggings in the neighborhood and she sensed the man was up to no good. But she had no choice—the only way to her apartment was to pass him.

"Guardian angel, protect me," Stacey murmured. "Be right beside me now and save me from harm."

With an outwardly confident stride, she looked straight ahead and went by the man. She could feel him looking at her, but he did nothing. It was all Stacey could do to keep from breaking into a run, but with her heart pounding, she managed to continue walking calmly until she had reached the corner. Then she raced the rest of the distance to her apartment building, ran up the stairs, and breathlessly locked the door behind her. It took a while for her to calm down. For some reason, she felt she had escaped a great danger.

A short time later, Stacey heard police sirens and, looking out her window, saw flashing red lights. Something was going on nearby, an accident or another mugging.

The following day on her way to work, she saw a neighbor. "What was all the excitement about last night?" Stacey asked.

"A rape," the woman told her grimly. "Just after six o'clock."

Stacey's mouth dropped. The rape had occurred on the very spot where she had passed the loitering man, just *before* six o'clock. What if he was the rapist? She had gotten a good look at him. Perhaps she could help the police with a description.

When she phoned, however, she discovered that the police had a suspect in custody. "Would you want to try to pick him out in a lineup?" a policeman asked her. "Your testimony could help place him at the scene."

Stacey agreed. That night she identified him as the man she had passed on her way home. "Why didn't he attack *me?*" she asked the policeman. "After all, I was just as vulnerable as the next woman who came along."

The policeman was curious too, and he agreed to describe Stacey to the suspect and ask him if he remembered her. Stacey never forgot his answer.

"I remember her. But why would I have bothered her?" the rapist asked. "She was walking down the street with two big guys, one on either side of her."

# Tender Touches

*...There was a shift of stars, a glimmering of blue light, and he felt himself surrounded by blueness and suspended. A moment later he was deposited, with a gentle bump, upon the rock....*

RAY BRADBURY, *"THE FIRE BALLOONS"*

The touch of love can be subtle, just a hint that someone else is there to help, just a small whisper or caress. Or it can be something physical but invisible. In some cases, this touch is firm, almost a grip—but with nothing seen, nothing "proved."

Jean Biltz was expecting her fifth child in a few months. On a cold spring morning she awakened in her Wichita home early and, after making the coffee, went outside to see if the milkman had made his delivery.

During the night the back porch had become glazed with ice, and as Jean stepped onto it, both her feet slipped out from under her. There was no railing on the stoop, nowhere to catch hold and keep herself from tumbling down the stairs. Almost in slow motion, Jean saw herself falling... falling... perhaps losing her unborn baby.

Then all of a sudden, two strong arms caught Jean and stood her up straight against the door. Thank heaven her husband had awakened early and was at the right place at the right time! Her grateful heart still pounding, she turned to him...but there was no one there at all. The door stood open, the kitchen beyond was empty, and even the snow-covered yard was silent, except for a little sigh in the wind.

Jean's baby was born strong and healthy, and today is the father of eight.

Someone touched little Tess with the same degree of protection. She and a friend had been playing in a Tennessee yard, and it was time for Tess to go home. Saying good-bye to her playmate, Tess ran toward a backyard precipice and took a flying leap across it, as she usually did when going home. But although her feet definitely left the ground, she felt hands on both her arms, pulling her firmly back, and she landed on *this* side of the ravine.

What was going on here? Puzzled, the child backed up and ran again, trying to jump the chasm a second time. Again the hands caught, held her, then set her gently down. But her playmate had gone in to dinner—and there was no one anywhere in view.

Perplexed, Tess walked to the edge of the ravine and looked across. There, coiled in the exact spot where she would have landed, was a rattlesnake.

The "tender touch" was even subtler for Emily Frank-Pogorzelski. It was early evening—a fatiguing and frustrating period of the day for all mothers—and Emily was preparing dinner. Diana, her toddler, was riding her toy horse around the kitchen. Several times Emily almost tripped over Diana and her clackety toy. Emily's patience was wearing thinner by the minute. Finally, in exasperation, she reached down to give the horse a hard push, to roll her daughter away from her.

"Suddenly I felt my whole arm stop in midair, like some sort of invisible block," Emily says. "I didn't feel another hand or a grip, but actual paralysis, which extended from my shoulder all the way down the upper extremity. I was aware that the power (or lack of it) was coming from something outside myself." Nor did her arm feel "asleep" or tingly; she could move it anywhere *except* toward Diana's horse.

Emily looked up, bewildered. And in one of those microseconds that seems eternal, she realized that the cellar door was open. Had she pushed Diana, the little girl would have shot across the floor, through the door—and down the steps to the stone floor below.

Mary Stebbins, another young mother, was also having an aggravating day, and her anger over a situation with some noisy neighbors was threatening to get out of control. Irritated, she huffed out of her bedroom and stomped down the hallway toward the kitchen. In her path was the open door to the basement, blocking her way. "As far as I can remember, none of the family was in the kitchen. In fact, I thought the area was deserted," she told me.

Wanting to vent her anger, Mary reached out to give the basement door a satisfying slam. But oddly, a strong pressure prevented her from doing so. The "pressure" seemed like a mass of invisible matter, a pillowy sort of "something" that gave an inch or two with the force of her hand, but then seemingly ran into *another* block, which thrust Mary's hand back. She simply could not finish the push.

Puzzled, Mary looked around the door, and gasped. There

was her two-year-old daughter at the top of the basement stairs. Had Mary slammed the door, it would have smacked the baby and, losing her balance, the child most likely would have plummeted down the stairs to the cement.

In every case, the recipients felt trembly as they realized what *could* have happened, then elated that everything was all right. Emily experienced an additional emotion: reassurance. "It was as if the wonderful being who stopped me from making a grave mistake was saying: 'Okay, you were impatient, but so what? Don't dwell on it. Go on from here.'

"I don't know if the being was my angel, my child's angel, or a combination," Emily says. "But there are times when I feel a loving spirit so close behind my right shoulder that I could touch her with my fingers. We are fortunate to have such spirits helping us—and sometimes saving us from ourselves."

# A Tiny Piece of Heaven

*I want to be an angel*
*And with the angels stand,*
*A crown upon my forehead,*
*A harp within my hand.*

URANIA BAILEY
*"I WANT TO BE AN ANGEL"*

*M*ost adults don't see an angel that resembles the typical rendition in art. Children, however, seem to connect with the winged and haloed version.

One mother and her little daughter were walking down the street when, a few feet from a wall, the child stopped. The mother urged her on, but the child seemed rooted to the spot. Suddenly there was a great crash—the wall had fallen. Had they gone on, they undoubtedly would have been crushed to death. Pale with fright, the woman asked her daughter why she had stopped at that precise moment.

"Didn't you see that beautiful man, dressed in a long white gown, Mommy?" the child asked. "He stood right in front of me so I could not go on." [10]

Jesus had special things to say about children. He wanted them to be able to come to him freely, unhindered by adults, because their innocence and pure hearts were what the kingdom of heaven was all about (Mark 10:14). Perhaps this is why little ones seem able to cut through the spiritual barriers we adults so often construct, and see a tiny piece of heaven. But when it happens, we adults still find it hard to believe.

That was the reaction of Laura Leigh Agnese of Bethpage, New York. Her then three-year-old son Danny was by all accounts an especially nice child, caring and honest, although he loved telling—and embellishing—stories. He also had his share of accidents.

One morning Danny tore across the living-room floor and tripped. A horrified Laura Leigh watched him, almost in slow motion, hurtle headfirst toward the sharp corner of a table. She took several steps, knowing already that she was too late to break his fall.

But Danny didn't hit the table at all. Instead, he seemed to stop in midair. Within a few seconds he stood straight up again and ran on.

Puzzled, Laura Leigh replayed the scene in her mind. Yes, he had certainly been falling straight toward the table, and a three-year-old, tumbling at that speed, wouldn't have enough control or agility to twist away. Nor had she noticed Danny trying to catch himself. Yet he had somehow stopped falling. The episode defied the law of gravity!

By the next day, Laura Leigh had forgotten the incident—until Danny, absorbed in play, looked up at her.

"Mommy? I saw a beautiful lady. With wings."

"Really, Danny?" Laura Leigh smiled. His stories were so imaginative. "What is the lady like?"

"She's nice," Danny said matter-of-factly. "She caught me yesterday so I didn't hit my head against the table."

Laura Leigh felt a chill. "Did the lady say anything?"

"Uh-huh. She said she was going to watch over me and keep me from getting hurt."

Danny went back to his toy, but Laura Leigh was lost in thought. "Danny was so little that my husband and I hadn't really taught him about spiritual things," she says. "We had told him about God, but we hadn't mentioned angels—we didn't know much about them ourselves." He'd had no exposure to angels through preschool, church, or television either, at least not that she knew. "Now Danny was telling me about a beautiful lady, and it seemed a perfect answer to an unexplainable event."

Yet Laura Leigh found it hard to believe her son. Children that age had trouble separating fact from fantasy, didn't they? And yet, he had seemed so certain. . . .

When her daughter was born, Laura Leigh had placed a print of a cherub over her crib. Now she went and got it. "Did your beautiful lady look like this, Danny?" she asked.

Danny looked at the picture of the baby angel, then at her, his eyes puzzled. "No, Mommy. That isn't a *lady*."

Laura Leigh didn't want to mention the word *angel*. "But it has wings. Don't they look just a little bit alike?"

Danny shook his head firmly. Although he usually enjoyed telling stories, this was different. Obviously, to him, the lady had been real.

Confused, Laura Leigh phoned her sister-in-law Roseann Sciaretta. Not only was Roseann a faith-filled woman, able to reassure Laura Leigh that angels were wonderful, she also knew Danny very well. "Danny wouldn't lie about a thing like that," Roseann comforted Laura Leigh. "But let me try something."

The next day Roseann brought a picture card of a guardian angel to Laura Leigh's home. The angel looked female and had large wings coming out of her shoulders. "Take a look at this, Danny," Roseann said, giving her nephew the picture.

Danny's eyes instantly lit up. "The lady!" he said, smiling. "Look, Mommy, that's the lady I saw! She's the friend that's going to watch over me! Can I keep this?"

Danny never mentioned the beautiful lady again, and today, four years later, has apparently forgotten the incident. But Danny also seems to be a remarkably kind and gentle boy, particularly interested in spiritual things. And the picture of the angel is still on his mirror.

# The Light of Love

*Because He is love in its essence, God appears before the angels ... as a sun. And from that sun, heat and light go forth; the heat being love and the light, wisdom. And the angels [become] love and wisdom, not from themselves but from the Lord.*

EMANUEL SWEDENBORG, *ANGELIC WISDOM*

Since angels are creatures of God, Who is the light of the world, a glow or even a flash of brilliant light is another signal of their presence. Malcolm Muggeridge, writing in *Something Beautiful for God*, the story of Mother Teresa of Calcutta, recounts an episode when the British Broadcasting Company was filming a documentary about her. The script called for some scenes within Mother Teresa's Home for the Dying, but it was dimly lit, with small high windows, and the photographer was certain that filming could not be done there. It was decided to try anyway, but just so the visit would not be a complete loss, the photographer also took some footage outside in the sunny courtyard.

When the film was processed, the part taken *inside* was bathed in a beautiful soft glow, whereas the part taken in the sunny courtyard was rather dim and confused. The film was checked and found to be perfectly adequate. Such a thing should not have happened.

"I am convinced that the technically unaccountable light

is, in fact, supernatural," Muggeridge wrote. "Mother Teresa's Home for the Dying is overflowing with a luminous love, like the haloes artists have seen and made visible.... I find it not at all surprising that the luminosity should register on a photographic film." [11]

This light of love is more common than we realize. Consider Chad and Peggy Anderson, who on a cold predawn Saturday were already bustling around the kitchen in their Antioch, Illinois, home. Peggy, a nurse, was due to work the seven-A.M.-to-three-P.M. shift at McHenry Hospital. And as any working wife knows, getting up, dressed, and *out* takes plenty of time. As he usually did when Peggy worked a Saturday shift, Chad would be caring for the Andersons' two sons as well as two preschool grandchildren currently living with them. Now, though, as he glanced outside, he frowned and said, "It's snowing, Peg."

"Not heavily." Peggy peered out the kitchen window.

"No...but I think you ought to drive the Lincoln rather than your little Chevette. Just in case."

"Well...." Peggy wasn't especially nervous in snow, but the hospital was twenty miles away, and she had to cover a rather zigzag, mostly rural route. The big car would be safer, so she decided to take Chad's advice.

The cold white blanket made everything look fresh and new, and although Peggy seemed the only traveler on the road, she was actually enjoying the ride—until she hit a curve on a bridge about eight miles from McHenry. The snow-covered pavement was slicker than she had assumed, and with the frozen marsh some thirty or forty feet below, Peggy attempted to slow down. Instead, the big car swerved and went into a 360-degree rotation. Peggy tensed immediately, trying frantically to remember what one was supposed to do to straighten a spinning car. But it was too late. She had lost control and the Lincoln was obviously going to plunge through the guardrail into the marsh below—there was nowhere else for it to go. Would she drown in a watery prison? Her little boys—what would become of them? "Oh, God," she called as the Lincoln veered toward the posts, "help me!"

There were no other vehicles in view, and Peggy's headlights were still the only illumination. But suddenly, in the dawn's semidarkness, a warm glow lit the spinning car's interior. At the same time, Peggy was filled with indescribable reassurance. The light warmed her, bathing her in contentment, and it was simply . . . heavenly. She knew—without exactly knowing *how* she knew—that there was no reason to be afraid.

And yes, the car was still going—but somehow approaching the end of the bridge without crashing through the rail, now rolling down the side of the steep thirty-foot ditch to the marshland below, now, unbelievably, slowing in a small clearing. It came to a stop. The light immediately went out.

"I sat in the car in amazement, just praying and praising God for a few minutes," Peggy recalls. "Then I got out and made my way up to the road."

The highway was still empty, but Peggy saw one house—the only one in view—all lit up and looking warm and inviting. The man who lived there was extremely hospitable and concerned about Peggy and her near miss. She phoned the hospital and her husband, blurting out the story as if she could not believe it herself. Chad sent a tow truck and came to fetch her in the little car, filled with children—and joy.

"Nothing like this ever happened to me before, and nothing quite as marvelous has happened since," says Peggy, who with her family now raises beef cattle on a small Nebraska farm. "But the experience gave me a deeper understanding of what total trust in God is all about." She still likes to tell people about the day an angel met her on a bridge—and gave her a glimpse of heaven.

# Angel in the Andes

*An angel stood and met my gaze,*
*Through the low doorway of my tent;*
*The tent is struck, the vision stays—*
*I only know she came and went.*

JAMES RUSSELL LOWELL
*"SHE CAME AND WENT"*

$\mathcal{B}$orn in 1900, Dr. Raymond Edman was a missionary, lecturer, professor of history, and, for twenty-five years, president of Wheaton College in Wheaton, Illinois, the alma mater of the Reverend Billy Graham and many other well-known Christian leaders. Dr. Edman wrote nineteen books and edited the *Alliance Witness*, but was probably best known for his deep devotion to God. "He was a mystic in the finest sense of the word," Billy Graham eulogized him at his funeral in 1967. "Part of his life was always in heaven."

Dr. Edman believed firmly that angels are involved in the world and that, occasionally, their work requires appearance in human form. During these times, "nothing about their dress or speech would make them different from others present," he said. "Only the discerning heart understands, and that usually long afterward, that the stranger who helped at a moment of emergency was really one of God's angels." As an example, in the *Wheaton College Bulletin*, Dr. Edman offered an experience of his own:

*   *   *

From 1923 to 1928, Edman and his wife were young missionaries in the Andes, Ecuador. They lived on the outskirts of the city where they could reach both the Spanish-speaking citizens as well as the shy, suspicious Indians who passed their doorway on the way to market.

But their assignment was difficult. "The people were unfriendly, and some were fanatical in their bitter opposition to our presence in their city," Edman recalled. "On occasion, small crowds would gather to hurl insults as well as stones. The Indians from the countryside were especially timid about being friendly with us because of intimidation by the townspeople. As a result, it was often difficult for us to shop for the bare necessities of life—fruits and vegetables, or charcoal for the kitchen stove." Perhaps more burdensome than physical hardships was loneliness. The young couple was never fearful, but with a complete lack of a support group—even one encouraging friend in this unfamiliar land—their emotional isolation must have been intense. And because of their awareness that some stranger might harass them or get into their house to steal, they kept the grilled gate on their high iron fence locked at all times, probably adding to their sense of disconnection.

The couple often fed hungry strangers or attempted to buy necessities from passing Indians, and one noon as they ate on their patio at the back of the house, they heard a rattling on the gate. When Edman went out with the key, he saw a barefoot Indian woman standing on the other side of the gate, one hand inside the bars knocking on the chain with the padlock. She wore beads and the large heavy hat of the mountain women, along with a dress of coarse woolen cloth and a brightly colored homemade belt. On her shoulders was a bundle, and a blue shawl, but she did not appear to have merchandise or food to sell. Edman hadn't seen her before.

As he approached, she began to speak softly in the mixture of Spanish and Quichua typical of the Indians who lived close to town. Pointing to a Gospel verse the Edmans had posted on the porch, she then asked, "Are you the people who have come to tell us about the living God?"

Edman was startled. No one had ever asked him that. "Yes, *Mamita* (little mother)," he answered. "We are."

The woman then raised the hand that was still inside the gate and began to pray—for blessings upon the couple's house, for their courage to follow His guidance, for joy in the task. Finally, she blessed Edman, withdrew her hand, smiled at him, eyes shining, then bowed and turned to go.

He had been so taken aback at her friendly support that he was speechless. Then, realizing that it was hot and the Indian woman should be invited inside to eat and rest, he quickly unlocked the gate and stepped through to call her back. In the time elapsed, she could not have gone more than five or ten yards in any direction. But she was not there.

"Where could she have gone so quickly? It was at least fifty yards from our gate to the corner of the street, and there was no opening along that stretch." Edman ran to the corner—assuming that if she had gotten that far, he could surely see her—but again, no woman, no passages into which she could have slipped. He went to the nearest open gate and asked two men repairing a wheel if an Indian woman had passed or come in.

They both looked up. "No, sir."

"I mean *just* now."

"Sir, we have been here for an hour or more," one answered, "and no one has entered or left during that time."

Edman hastened back to the corner, but there was not a soul in sight. Thoughtfully he returned home and told his wife about the matter.

For the next several days, Edman remained strangely moved and peaceful concerning his formidable assignment. There seemed to be a sweet and indefinable aroma surrounding him, something that did not come from the flowers in his garden. It was only later that he gradually pieced together the meaning of it all. "I began to understand that the Almighty had none of His earthly servants at hand to encourage two young missionaries, so He was pleased to send an angel from heaven," Edman concluded. "Over the many years since then, during all of life's deep testing, there has remained the glow of God's blessing, pronounced by someone who looked exactly like an old Quichua Indian woman." [12]

# *The Hands of a Comforter*

*Who does the best [her] circumstance allows*
*Does well, acts nobly; angels could do no more.*
EDWARD YOUNG, *NIGHT THOUGHTS*

*M*illions of people watch the wholesome family fare on cable television's Eternal Word Television Network. The unlikely founder of EWTN, Mother Mary Angelica, is a Catholic cloistered nun who, with a handful of other sisters, two hundred dollars, and absolutely no knowledge of television ("Okay," Mother Angelica concedes, "so I did know how to turn one on.") has become the only woman in religious television who owns a network.

Visitors to the EWTN complex outside Birmingham, Alabama, cannot help but be impressed with what God and this little nun have accomplished. A monastery, network facilities and satellite dish, a print shop and chapel stand incongruously in the midst of the Protestant Bible Belt. When Mother Angelica believed in 1981 that God was calling her to begin a media ministry, she simply did so, and everything else has fallen into place.

Mother Angelica doesn't take herself too seriously, which is probably why viewers choose her twice-weekly show, "Mother Angelica Live," as their favorite. Although it features a studio audience, call-ins from across the country, and popular guests, the show is sometimes less than polished. Sets occasionally collapse, for example, and Mother Angelica is prone to fits of giggles and witty asides.

Despite her grandmotherly image, she is firm and no-nonsense in her views on morality, yet quick to encourage and express compassion. Often, she ministers on the air to anonymous callers, counseling a distraught divorcee, gently scolding a drug addict, bringing God's healing "to those who, perhaps, can't reach out any other way."

"I want to be a thorn in people's sides," she admits. "I want to challenge them; I want to be another John the Baptist who says, 'Get with it!'"

Fewer viewers know, perhaps, that Mother Angelica, who was born Rita Rizzo, had a rough childhood. After a bitter marriage, her parents divorced when she was six. Little Rita was poverty-stricken, vulnerable, and, because of her mother's divorce, ostracized within her Canton, Ohio, church community. Nor was she particularly impressed with the nuns. "I remember sitting in church watching them pray, and vowing I would never be among their ranks," Mother Angelica says. "Their facial expressions were sour, their headpieces too large—I was convinced they were the most unhappy people I'd ever seen." Then one day she experienced a moment of grace, a touch meant especially for her.

Mother Angelica has told the story often. About eleven years old, and feeling especially lonely and sad, she was walking downtown one evening, oblivious to everything around her. "I started to cross a busy street, then heard a woman's shrill scream behind me," she recalls. Rita looked back expecting to see someone in trouble, and instead realized that a car was speeding toward her, the headlights shining in her eyes. There was no time to get to the safety island. Rita froze, closed her eyes, and waited for the fatal impact.

Instead she felt two strong hands lift her high in the air. A moment later she blinked and looked around in disbelief. She was standing on the sidewalk!

A crowd gathered. Onlookers had expected to see a terrible accident and a child's crumpled body. Instead they found a healthy, but quite frightened, girl. To them, it appeared that she had definitely been hit, then hurled aside by the force of the collision. They were completely mystified at her lack of injuries.

A bus driver who witnessed the event from his higher perch later reported, with disbelief, a somewhat different scenario. He insisted that Rita had jumped or somehow been catapulted high into the air, easily clearing both the safety island and the onrushing auto. Such a feat seemed impossible, and the man was dumbfounded.

As soon as she got home, Rita told her mother what had happened, and both of them gave thanks for this rare moment of joy. Somehow they understood that, despite their hardships, they were being guided and cared for.

That was the beginning of Rita's confidence in angels. When she entered the Poor Clares convent, she chose a new name that would honor them. Later she founded (and named) Our Lady of the Angels Monastery, where she still lives, writes books, and directs her television network. Her life has been a testimony to the power of faith.

But Mother Angelica hasn't forgotten that extraordinary moment when she felt the hands of a comforter and knew that God's love would never fail.

# Bedside Companion

*What know we of the Blest above*
*But that they sing, and that they love?*
WORDSWORTH
*"SCENE ON THE LAKE OF BRIENZ"*

*It* was the Labor Day weekend, and Sandy Smith (now Waters) would soon be leaving for her first year of college. Her mother had died the previous spring, and Sandy was still raw over the loss, apprehensive about the transition from high school to a university. She and her friend Bobbie decided to drive to Hocking Hills State Park in southern Ohio to camp, a "last fling" before saying good-bye to summer.

The girls were on Interstate 23 when Sandy, who has a heart condition, experienced some angina pain. "I swerved over the gravel on the roadside," Sandy recalls. "Then, trying to turn back, I swung the wheel too far. The car flipped and rolled over several times down a small hill." Sandy was sure that she was going to die. "I saw the whole scene in slow motion, just like other survivors have mentioned," she says. "But I fainted before the car stopped."

Miraculously, only Sandy's nose was broken, but blood was everywhere. Bobbie, who had remained conscious, managed to wedge open the passenger door and stumble up to the highway, where she flagged down a trucker.

When Sandy awoke at the Delaware Memorial Hospital, she was in a bed in a secluded alcove. How badly was she hurt? Was Bobbie all right? She looked at herself, shocked to see dried blood all over her clothes and arms. Filled with loneliness and fear, she started to cry.

"All I wanted was my mother," Sandy says. "I cried out for her to come and hold me. But she was dead, and no one came."

Sandy fainted again, and the next time she awakened, there was a person sitting next to her, stroking her hand in the most comforting way. "I'm not positive it was a woman, and it hurt too much to turn my head, but I could tell that she had long, almost-white hair and pale skin," Sandy says. "Her clothing was white too, but I couldn't see if she was wearing pants or a skirt."

With the soothing sensation of a protective hand on hers, Sandy calmed down. A noise seemed to be coming from the figure, a fanlike whirring but deeper, like the beating of thousands of birds' wings. Sandy felt an overwhelming sense of peace and love. The love actually seemed to flow from the noise the figure made, filling the lonely room.

"The noise sounded like a song, not in a conventional sense, but almost like millions of voices blending together in the most extraordinary tones.... This is difficult to discuss. I know it was not a psychological experience. Nor was I hallucinating because I had been injured. I felt it was a supernatural being who had come to comfort me. And I had a serenity so profound that it was impossible to explain."

As the figure hummed, Sandy fell into a restful sleep, and when she awoke for the third time, a nurse was washing her face. Sandy assumed the nurse was her "figure in white."

"When you finish, could you hold my hand?" Sandy asked. "Like you did before?"

The nurse looked puzzled. "No one's been holding your hand," she said.

"Yes, a blond lady in white did," Sandy said. "I thought it was you. Didn't you sit next to me and sing?"

"I wouldn't have had time," the nurse explained. "It's Labor Day weekend, and we're extremely short of help."

"But someone . . ." Sandy began.

"It must have been a dream," the nurse soothed. "You see, I've been right outside this alcove ever since they brought you in, and no one's been near you. Everyone in the emergency room has been caring for your friend and the other patients. And there are no fair-haired nurses on duty today."

Sandy didn't ask again. She was beginning to realize that her visitor had been someone out of the ordinary, perhaps sent at a time when she was so emotionally overwhelmed, so needy for her mother that only a special being could bring the consolation she needed.

"It was a pivotal point in my life," Sandy says today. "I was going through a spiritual rebellion, questioning whether there was a God, reading a lot of philosophy. My visitor changed the way I thought about religion. She also restored my faith that life could be good again, despite my mother's death. The tranquility she left with me remained for a long time."

Sandy has experienced many moments of joy since then. Only rarely has she reached this indescribable peace—and when she does, she knows her angel is near. One significant moment was the morning of her wedding day when she heard the familiar humming noise fill her room.

"This must be how we'll feel in heaven," Sandy says. She has developed a real affinity for angels and looks for them everywhere. "I suspect I've come across others, even if I didn't recognize them," she says. "And I'm certain I'll meet my special comforter again."

# Twice Blessed

*Praise the Lord, you his angels,*
*you mighty ones who do his bidding,*
*who obey his word.*

PSALMS 103:20

It's logical to assume that recipients of heavenly touches probably rank just a little lower than angels themselves. "I'm not especially holy," most of us would conclude. "Spirits wouldn't appear to *me*."

Yet we ought not to second-guess these blessed helpers. After all, if their job is to minister to humankind to bring us closer and closer to God, why would anyone be exempt?

Bob Lessnau had been raised in a Christian home, but had given up trying to please God by the time he was sixteen. "As a typical adolescent, I figured I was always offending God with one sin or another," Bob says. "I decided to put religion behind me."

Bob served in Vietnam, returned to Michigan, became a telephone repairman, married and had three children. "During those years I began to reflect on the close calls I'd had in Vietnam. I'd felt protected then, and thought maybe I ought to reevaluate my relationship with God," Bob says. "Even a dunce could see that not only was God *not* looking for an excuse to toss me into hell, He was doing everything He could to keep me alive so I could come to my senses!"

Bob hadn't gotten around to acting on his good intention on the day he entered the Big Boy on Biddle Street in Wyandotte, Michigan. The restaurant was busy but not crowded, and Bob had a good view of his surroundings. He sat at the counter and ordered lunch. No one he knew was in the restaurant, and strangers were sitting on the stools on either side of him.

Bob didn't see anyone approach. But suddenly a scholarly-looking man in a suit tapped him on the shoulder. Bob swung around on the stool.

The man looked at Bob. "I want to see you in church," he said. Although he wasn't shouting, his voice could certainly be heard by everyone in the immediate vicinity.

Bob was dumbfounded and embarrassed. "Why me? Although I wasn't going to church at that time—and was still smoking pot and behaving in less than holy ways—I wasn't wearing a sign announcing any of it," he says. "I decided the guy was some kind of nut soliciting for his church. But I didn't live in Wyandotte, and I told him so."

"I didn't say *what* church," the man replied. "I said I want to see you *in* church."

Bob swiveled away for just a few seconds, to mull over the strange comment, then turned back. "I wanted to ask him how he knew I wasn't going to church."

But the man was no longer behind Bob. In fact, Bob couldn't see him anywhere. It had only been a few seconds— he couldn't have made it to the door in just that time, Bob notes, "not unless he had broken into a run, which certainly would have attracted the attention of the customers." But he was gone.

Everything else was just the same. People kept eating and talking. Those on either side of Bob seemed not to have noticed or overheard anything peculiar. Had Bob been the only person in the restaurant to see and hear the visitor?

That night, Bob discussed the incident with his wife, Sandy. "We decided that if God wanted us in church so much that He would go to all this trouble, we ought to give it some thought." The couple worried that their noisy preschoolers would bother other worshipers, but they joined an Assembly of God church anyway. Bob decided to give up marijuana, found his spiritual life flourishing, and developed a fellowship with other couples.

And he and Sandy needn't have worried about their little ones. "The children were fine. They sat there obediently, week after week," Bob recalls. "Just like little angels."

But God hadn't finished with Bob. Several years later, he was in his driveway, working on a friend's 1971 Dodge Dart. The car was facing up a slight incline. Bob was lying under it in the gas-tank area, feet pointing toward its front. His friend had gone to the store to buy a replacement part.

"I had forgotten that removing the drive shaft gives you, in essence, four freewheeling wheels," Bob explains. "Though the car was set in 'park,' it started to roll backward."

Bob attempted to scurry out from under. He almost made it, but the front wheel caught his left foot, pinning it by bending it forward toward the shin. His heart dropping, Bob saw that the slant in the driveway was enough to make the car roll, but not enough for the wheel to complete its revolution over his foot. He was stuck.

Pain exploded in waves. His foot felt as if it were being

crushed into bits. Alerted by his shouts, Sandy and a neighbor woman came running.

"We'll lift the wheel, Bob, and then you can get out!" Sandy cried.

But their efforts only made matters worse. Because of the incline, every time the women tried to shift the tire, they only pushed it farther up, resting even more weight on Bob's whole leg. If the wheel could have turned *completely* over the foot, Bob could have gotten free, but it wouldn't move far enough.

Soon there were at least seven other neighbors surrounding him. Some tried the same type of lifting, to no avail. "Everyone should have pushed the wheel from behind," Bob says in retrospect, "but none of us was thinking clearly." It seemed as if he would be trapped forever. Through a haze of pain and fear, Bob cried out, "God, help me!"

Immediately, Bob saw a large man running toward him. The man reached the front of the car and quickly lifted the bumper high enough to raise the entire chassis off Bob's foot. Bob groaned in relief and rolled free.

Everyone crowded around.

"Are you okay?" someone asked. "Should we take you for an X ray?"

"No." Experimentally, Bob wiggled his toes and flexed his ankle. The foot had no apparent injury. "It feels fine," he told his relieved neighbors, getting up slowly.

Then Bob looked around for the large man who had so effortlessly lifted the car. "I was beginning to realize just how strong he would have had to be," he says. "Allowing for the 'springiness' of the car springs, lifting a car ten or twelve inches would still leave a tire on the ground. You'd have to lift it a lot higher than that to get a wheel completely off a foot. And there was no one else lifting on that side when he came."

There was no large man for Bob to thank, either. And no one remembered seeing him dash to Bob's aid. "The tall guy, the one who came running across the lawn ... ?" Bob asked everyone, but was rewarded with stares and head-shaking.

"There was no one here but us," the neighbors insisted, "and we would certainly have noticed a stranger." Nor did Sandy remember seeing anyone she didn't know.

There were no service vehicles around, no deliverymen or any outsiders on Bob's street that afternoon. No one had seen a car stop. More significantly, no one had seen or heard a car *leave*. There just wasn't any explanation as to why the car had suddenly moved off Bob's foot. Any *logical* explanation, that is.

"I'm ninety-nine percent certain that he was an angel, because of the timeliness of his approach, his extraordinary strength, and his quick vanishing act," Bob says. In fact, even though the muscular stranger bore no resemblance to the bookish messenger in the Big Boy restaurant, Bob believes they could have both been sent from heaven.

Why isn't Bob one hundred percent sure? "Maybe because it leaves room for faith," he explains. "I have a choice. I can write these experiences off to good luck. Or give God the credit."

Bob has chosen God.

# He Will Send Angels

*How many angels are there? One—*
*who transforms our life—is plenty.*
TRADITIONAL SAYING

*T*here are many points of view about guardian angels. Some scholars believe that each of us may have two. But in telling the following story, Hope Price of Portland, Oregon, obviously believes that one is indeed plenty.

If it is true that we each have a guardian angel, then mine has been seen three times that I know of—each time by a different person.

My mother, Minnie Metcalf Miller, said that when I was three weeks old, and very tiny because I was premature, she was awakened in the night by a beautiful young girl bending over her.

Mother somehow understood from this beautiful visitor that her new baby, asleep in the next room, needed her. Mother also seemed to know that she would be facing a long ordeal, so she dressed carefully and went in to me. She found me blue in the face and struggling for breath.

There followed a long battle with pneumonia in which Mother did not have her clothes off for several nights. She said the beautiful girl was there beside her every minute of the fight with death.

A kind neighbor also saw the girl and asked my mother, "Who is the beautiful lady staying with you since the baby has been so sick? I see her come out on the front porch sometimes." The beautiful lady disappeared when I was completely out of danger.

Years later, in 1934, she returned to rescue me again. I now had small children of my own and had just gotten a divorce. I had been told by my doctor that I must have a serious operation, and an intensely religious woman named Lude was doing my housework. She was to stay with my three young children while I went to the hospital.

However, Lude seemed dissatisfied with conditions in our house, as she was used to working in wealthy households with other servants. One afternoon, as Lude entered the room with a vacuum cleaner, a cat, who was calling on my cat, jumped through the window, breaking the glass. This was the last straw for Lude. She gave notice rather sulkily, saying she would leave in the morning as she simply couldn't stay on.

I wondered what I would do! I couldn't leave three little children alone in the house while I was in the hospital. I finally decided I would have to call the doctor the next morning and tell him I could not have the operation.

However, early next morning Lude entered my room fairly beaming with good humor. She was wearing a white uniform. "Breakfast is ready," she smiled.

"Why, Lude, how nice of you to get breakfast before you go," I said.

"Mrs. Price," Lude replied, "I've changed my mind. I'm not going. I had a vision last night. A beautiful young girl, an angel, came flying in to my bedside through that window the cat broke. She was all in shining white and surrounded with light. It lit up my whole room. She asked me not to leave you because you needed me. I'm going to stay just as long as you need me."

So I went to the hospital comforted by the thought that the children were safely watched over by Lude.

In each case the angel was seen by a kind person with a good deal of spiritual understanding. They were the kind of persons able to see angels, obviously.

The lovely angel seems to appear when I need her most. I hope she always will. Perhaps some day I will see her myself.[13]

# Callers in the Night

*Angels, as 'tis but seldom they appear,*
*So neither do they make long stay;*
*They do but visit and away.*

JOHN NORRIS
*"TO THE MEMORY OF HIS NIECE"*

Angels do many things for us, but one of their primary jobs is to bring help, just when we need it most. I read of an incident involving a Philadelphia neurologist, Dr. S. W. Mitchell, who was awakened after a tiring day by a little girl knocking on his door. The child, poorly dressed and deeply upset, told him that her mother was sick and needed a physician.

Dr. Mitchell followed the child through the snowy night and found the mother desperately ill with pneumonia. After arranging for medical care, he complimented the sick woman on the intelligence and persistence of her little daughter. The woman looked at him strangely, and then said, "My daughter died a month ago."

Dr. Mitchell, amazed and perplexed, went to the closet and opened the door. There hung the coat worn by the little girl who had led him to her mother. Despite the wintry night, the coat was completely dry.[14]

\* \* \*

And then there is the account of Father O'Keeffe of Cork, Ireland, who was summoned by a handsome young man to attend a woman who was dying. The priest followed the man into a poor section of Cork in which nothing could be seen but ramshackle stables. "Where on earth is this person to be found?" he asked his guide.

"We are near the place now, Father," the young man said, ånd instantly disappeared.

The priest was astonished and at a loss, until he heard groans nearby and found a young woman dying on a dunghill. She told him that her family had been well-to-do and she had attended a convent school where the sisters had told her to call on her guardian angel if she was ever in need.

The woman had gone on to live a wretched debauched life and now, abandoned and left to die alone, she had remembered her early teaching and had begged her guardian angel to bring her a priest.[15]

I learned of a similar incident in Chicago. In the late 1870s, Father Arnold Damien of the Society of Jesus founded Holy Family Church, which still stands just west of the University of Illinois's Circle Campus on Roosevelt Road. Father Damien was an outstanding preacher and traveled extensively. He also developed a large altar-boy society in Holy Family parish. Through the latter days of the nineteenth century, hundreds of Chicago youths were taught to assist the priests at mass.

Years passed, Father Damien aged and slipped into semi-retirement. On one especially raw and windy night, two young boys came to the Holy Family rectory where Father Damien lived, and rang the bell. Their grandmother was terribly sick, they explained to the porter when he answered the door, and she needed a priest to prepare her for death.

"It's too cold and rainy tonight," the porter told the youngsters. "We'll send a priest in the morning."

But Father Damien had heard the bell ring, and he went to the boys. "I'll go with you at once," he told them. "Come in and get warm while I go to the church for Holy Communion."

Father Damien followed the boys through the cold and desolate streets. They led him at last to a far corner of the parish, over a mile from the rectory. "She's up there in the attic rooms, Father," said one, pointing to a dilapidated building.

The priest ascended the narrow, dark stairs. Indeed, the door on the top floor was open. Entering the darkened apartment, he found an elderly woman, ill, cold, and close to death. Quickly, he anointed her and gave her Holy Communion for her journey into eternity. "Father," she whispered as the blessing was finished, "how did you happen to come? Only a few neighbors know I've been sick, and none are Catholic."

"Why, your grandsons brought me here to you," the priest explained.

The woman closed her eyes. "I had two grandsons, Father," she said, "and they were altar boys at Holy Family Church. But they both died, many years ago."

Were the little messengers angels? Father Damien believed so. And to mark this heavenly visitation, he had statues of two acolytes, holding candles and facing each other, placed high on either side of the entrance to the church's sanctuary, where they still stand.

# A Voice from Beyond

*The angels . . . regard our safety, undertake our defense, direct our ways and exercise a constant solicitude that no evil befalls us.*

JOHN CALVIN
*INSTITUTES OF THE CHRISTIAN RELIGION, VOLUME I*

*M*argaret walked the dog every morning; her husband, Paul (not their real names), did so at night. There was a small park across the busy street in front of their house, and Paul usually took the dog there. He was a reserved man who enjoyed solitude and rarely showed his emotions.

About nine one April evening, Paul and the dog started out on their customary jaunt. "I'm never in the garage after dinner," Margaret relates. "But that night, I happened to go there for something. The garage door was open and even though it was almost dark outside, I had a perfect view of Paul going down our driveway to the sidewalk."

Paul had to wait a few moments until there was a break in the traffic. While he was standing there, Margaret heard a voice calling. "Paul!" it said. That was all.

"It was a male voice, the kindest-sounding voice I'd ever heard," she says. "There is shrubbery alongside our driveway, and I assumed our next-door neighbor, hidden from my view by the garage wall and the foliage, was calling Paul.

"But I know his voice, and this wonderful voice was not his. A second later I remembered that the neighbor wasn't home."

Paul did not appear to have heard the voice. Maybe it had been her imagination. Or the sound of the wind? But there was no wind. Someone in a passing car? But the voice had been coming from her direction, as if the caller was near.

Puzzled, Margaret wondered what, if anything, she should do. Again, as her husband started to step down from the curb, the kind voice called his name. "Paul!"

Now Margaret saw Paul stop. Had he heard the voice this time?

Incredibly, a large tree in the park started to fall. Down it came, almost in slow motion, until, with a loud crash, it came to rest across the park path, its highest branches lying almost into the street. The spot was where Paul always walked, where he would have been at that moment had a voice not delayed him. Stunned, Margaret stared at the tree. Paul, in his usual unemotional manner, crossed the street, went around the tree, looked at it for a moment, and continued on his way. But by the time he returned he had had a chance to think.

"Someone called my name," he said to Margaret. "It happened twice. Did you hear the voice?"

"Yes. I wondered if you had."

"But there wasn't anyone around. Unless you saw someone."

"No, I didn't," Margaret told him. "And from the garage, I would have had a good view." They looked at each other.

"Well, then," Paul said in his usual calm fashion, "it had to have been my guardian angel."

Margaret replayed the episode in her mind many times, and her husband told several neighbors and relatives about it. But neither of them ever found anyone to thank.

# Master Builders

*What's impossible to all humanity may be possible*
*to the metaphysics and physiology of angels.*

JOSEPH GLANVILL
*THE VANITY OF DOGMATIZING*

$\mathscr{I}$n the mid-1800s, a courageous little band of Catholic nuns journeyed by paddleboat and covered wagon from Kentucky to sun-bleached Sante Fe, New Mexico, to establish a school. Their new surroundings were desolate, the people mainly Native Americans and Mexicans, and while the Sisters of Loretto learned the Spanish language and became acclimated, they lived in a tiny adobe house. Over time, Mexican carpenters built them a larger convent, a school, and an adobe chapel.

Eventually the little church became too small for the burgeoning community, and in 1873 work began on a larger stone building. In honor of their founding bishop's French background, Loretto Chapel would be the first Gothic structure west of the Mississippi. Impressively large by Southwestern standards, it would measure some twenty-five feet by seventy-five feet, reach a height of eighty-five feet, and have a choir loft at the rear.

The work progressed well until it was nearly finished—and the sisters realized that a formidable error had been made. There was no way to climb from the chapel floor to the choir loft. A staircase or connecting link had been inadvertently left out of the plans. Mother Magdalen, superior of the group, consulted several expert carpenters, but their verdict was the same: a staircase was impossible. The loft was exceptionally high, so an ordinary passageway would take up too much room. There were only two alternatives: climb to the loft via a ladder, which few of the sisters could imagine doing; or tear the whole balcony down and rebuild it, which would be a financial disaster.

In typical faith-fashion, the sisters decided to take no immediate action, and simply to pray and wait. They made a novena, a nine-day prayer, to St. Joseph, the patron of carpenters, and asked for a workable—and, one would presume, inexpensive—solution.

On the last day of the novena, a gray-haired man approached the convent, leading a donkey and carrying a tool chest.

"I've heard about your problem with the chapel," he told Mother Magdalen. "Would you let me try to build a staircase?"

"By all means," Mother Magdalen responded. She must have wondered how he could do it. According to later reports, the man had only a hammer, a saw, and a T square. There is no evidence that he ordered any wood, either, but some witnesses reported seeing tubs of water sitting around, filled with pieces of soaking board.

Accounts differ as to how long the actual work took—some say six to eight months—but eventually the man disappeared. Mother Magdalen went to pay him, but he was nowhere to be found. Nor did the local lumberyard have knowledge of the project or any bill for materials. To this day, there is no record that the job was ever paid for.

But what a job it was! For when the sisters went to inspect the chapel, they found a graceful spiral staircase linking the loft to the first floor, cleverly designed to take up a minimum of space. It is constructed only with pegs—no nails. Each stair is made out of several pieces and is perfectly curved and fitted. The unit makes two complete 360-degree turns, but since it has no supporting center pole or anchor for the sides of the treads, it should have long ago collapsed. Experts have failed to identify the wood, but it is definitely *not* a variety native to the New Mexico area. Where did the carpenter get it? With the exception of some brief modifications and an added banister, the staircase remains today as it was completed over one hundred years ago, a marvel of design unexplainable to the many architects, engineers, and construction experts who visit the site.

The sisters, of course, remain mum on *who* the considerate contractor was—it would be speculation at best. But he left behind a holy place, and their community is forever grateful.

A similar event took place in Covington, Kentucky. In 1938, the Reverend Maurice Coers and his wife traveled to the Holy Land, where they were deeply moved by a visit to a tomb reputed to be the authentic burial place of Jesus. Someday, Reverend Coers decided, he would build a replica of that sepulcher in America. It would be a sacred spot for people of all faiths who could not afford to visit the Holy Land site.

By the mid-1950s, Reverend Coers was a minister at the Immanuel Baptist Church in Covington, and he shared his dream with the congregation. The plan received enthusiastic support, and Reverend Coers found the perfect setting, a beautiful hill overlooking the Ohio River. Although the owner at first balked at selling the property, he eventually agreed. People from all over Covington contributed, and plans expanded to include a reproduction of a first-century carpenter shop, a chapel, and a bookstore. Coers named it The Garden of Hope.

The tomb and garden had been completed—and churches were already holding devotional services on the patio in front of the sepulcher's entrance—when difficulties developed. During the winter of 1958, the hillside began to give way, causing expensive landscaping, walkways, and the patio itself to slip downward. "The following summer, the church borrowed forty thousand dollars to sink cement pilings into the earth and pour tons of concrete onto the base of the hill," recalls one longtime parishioner. Workmen rebuilt the patio too and shored it up with more concrete.

But during the following winter, the entire area, including the patio, slid all the way to the bottom again. Distinguished engineers came to evaluate the church's predicament, but their verdicts were the same: The Garden of Hope could not be safely constructed on this site. However, there was no money left to begin elsewhere. "It was heartbreaking," Maurice Coers' widow says today. "The Garden of Hope had been a dream come true for Maurice, and now it looked impossible."

On a hot August day in 1959, several church members stood in the garden, dispiritedly surveying the situation. What could they do? Take out more trees? Rebuild? Pour even more concrete at the hill's base? Or should the project be abandoned?

No one took notice of a stranger making his way through

the garden until he stood in front of them. "I'm looking for Reverend Coers," the man said.

The others looked at him. He was huge, surely over three hundred pounds, and wearing bib overalls. Someone ran and got the minister.

"Hear you have a landslide going on here," the large man began.

"We do," Reverend Coers agreed. "The earth down there is full of concrete and steel pilings, but nothing seems to keep the hill—and everything on it—from sliding."

"Show it all to me," the man suggested.

Reverend Coers, impressed with the large man's dignity and air of quiet confidence, did so, while the rest of the men continued talking and wandering around. But when the minister returned from the brief tour, he was excited. The man in the overalls, it seemed, was an engineer who had had experience with railroad construction, particularly in the mountainous areas of the West. "He told me to write everything down, and I did," Reverend Coers told the others, waving sheets of paper. "We apparently need workmen to construct a certain kind of wall, like railroads use, to retain hillsides...." Reverend Coers was filled with rekindled enthusiasm and joy. No one noticed that the man in the bib overalls had disappeared.

Workmen were hired, and the retaining wall was completed ahead of schedule. But would it hold?

Winter weather arrived, with an onslaught of cold rarely experienced in Kentucky. Freezing and thawing was almost a daily routine, and Covington held its collective breath. The wall could not have been tested more severely. But not a foot of dirt moved, despite the elements.

Today the Covington hillside has become a popular pilgrimage spot, and the chapel is busy with weddings, worship services, and seminars. The tools in the carpenter shop are many centuries old and were donated by Israel's Prime Minister David Ben-Gurion. A piece of the Wailing Wall, a flag from Egypt, and a stone from the hillside on which Christ preached the Sermon on the Mount mingle with stained glass and statues donated by churches of various denominations; the project is truly an ecumenical venture.

Few visitors, perhaps, notice the retaining wall, although an occasional engineer marvels at its unique structure and design. But no one can explain who was responsible for it. For the considerate contractor never submitted a bill to the church board. Nor was he a member of any engineering fraternity, or listed among the certified engineers in the United States or, despite his imposing appearance, ever seen in the area again.

But, like the spiral staircase in Sante Fe, the wall speaks silently but powerfully of things unseen.

# Julia's Visitor

*He heard an odd noise, as though of a whirring . . .*
*and when he strained for a wider view, could have*
*sworn he saw a dark figure born aloft on a pair of*
*strong black wings.*

BERNARD MALAMUD, *"ANGEL LEVINE"*

*E*leanor Duffin of Justice, Illinois, shared a story handed down to the family by her mother, who was born in 1884.

A conscientious woman, Julia Zulaski devoted much time to teaching her children about spiritual matters. In the mornings before she dressed Eleanor and her three siblings, Julia would help them ask their angels to keep them safe. At night, Julia would tuck the children into a large double bed, turn off the light, then kneel in the semidarkness and pray for them.

"Since we four had been born in less than four years, we were all little and fit two at each end," Eleanor says. The children felt snug and safe, watching their mother pray beside them.

One night, after Eleanor and her siblings had fallen asleep, Julia remained on her knees in the darkened room. As she prayed, she noticed that the bedroom wall that held a window was beginning to glow. Was there something shining outside? Before she could get to her feet and investigate, the wall became luminous, more intensely bright.

Then the startled young woman saw a large angel fly through the closed window. He looked strong, powerful, and just like the pictures of angels Julia had seen in books. For a moment, he seemed to hover protectively over the bed where the four children slept. Then, as Julia watched in awed silence, he flew across the room and out through the other wall, and the room darkened once more.

"My mother didn't tell me about this until I was a teenager," Eleanor says, "and once she had told me, she never mentioned it again." It was as if such a memory was too precious to put into words, especially if others could not comprehend its majesty and meaning.

Julia Zulaski had a happy life, spending much of her time in cheerful service to others. Perhaps she knew that she had little to worry about. Her angel, after all, was nearby.

# The Gray Lady

*In this dim world of clouding cares,*
*We rarely know till 'wildered eyes*
*See white wings lessening up the skies,*
*The angels with us unawares.*

GERALD MASSEY
*"BALLAD OF BABY CHRISTABEL"*

$\mathcal{A}$ngelic rescues are sometimes dramatic. But they can also come softly, in such a tender manner that the one being helped is unaware of the supernatural aspect until some time has passed. Jean Doktor of Oceanside, California, knows this very well.

In 1980, Jean's husband, John, was struck by a strange illness. He had been a healthy sixty-year-old, jogging every day, but after returning from a business trip he ran a mild fever, which soon soared to 105 degrees. John's physician gave him antibiotics, but by the next day the fever had not broken and John was acting strange. "Whenever I spoke to John, I seemed to hear two voices in his response," Jean recalls. One was the familiar tones of her husband, now vague and wandering. Seemingly underlying *that* voice, however, was another, this one deep and comforting, which Jean seemed to hear saying, "You will get through this, John."

Jean called the doctor again, reporting not only the symptoms but the two-voiced phenomenon. "He must be hallucinating because of the high fever," the doctor told Jean. "Get him to the hospital right away."

Jean did, and although the diagnosis was pneumonia, John soon rallied and was sent home. But the strange symptoms reappeared, and by the time John had been rushed again to the hospital, he had fallen into a semiconscious state. "The doctor told us that John could hear our voices, but could not respond to us—instead, he would repeat every word we said to him," Jean says. "It was a nightmare. My healthy reliable husband was failing right in front of me."

During the next few days, John faded in and out of awareness. Four specialists entered the case. They took spinal taps and blood cultures, even checked the possibility of chemical poisoning, but remained baffled. Nothing seemed to work—and there was nothing more to do.

By Saturday night, the Doktors' three grown children had gathered in their father's room, shocked at his deteriorating condition. Jean wept quietly with fear and exhaustion. It seemed obvious that John was slipping away from them, and she could do nothing at all to help. "Please God," she prayed, as she held his limp and unresponsive hand, "let me keep my husband. I need him...I love him...."

On Sunday morning, Jean was alone in the room, watching John's drawn and pallid face. There was a knock, and she rose to face an elderly lady dressed stylishly in gray silk, her white hair beautifully arranged. She was carrying a little gold container holding communion hosts, and Jean assumed she was what Catholics term a "lay minister," someone who brings the Eucharist to hospital patients.

"Get Brother John on his feet," the woman told Jean in a firm but friendly tone.

Brother John? Who *was* this person? Jean was sure that a lay minister would never interfere with a patient's routine. "That's impossible," she protested. "My husband can't move."

"He needs to stand up," the gray lady repeated in a gentle but reproving tone. Jean was irritated at the woman's high-handedness. What if the floor nurse came in and found them disturbing John? Yet Jean also felt compelled to obey this brisk but oddly reassuring stranger, so much so that she suddenly reached for her husband and pulled him to a sitting position. The woman looked on, composed and quiet.

John was groggy, but he didn't protest Jean's efforts, and somehow, with her support, the two of them stood swaying. Then the gray lady gripped both their hands, and waves of cold electricity shot through Jean.

"We earnestly request the healing of Brother John," the gray lady murmured, "and may the love of Jesus touch him. May he be instantly healed."

She placed the wafer on John's tongue, snapped the little gold box shut, turned, and briskly left the room. Jean helped John into bed, where he immediately fell into a deep sleep.

*That* had been an odd episode, Jean mused. She was fortunate that hospital personnel hadn't caught her dragging John out of bed! But it had been nice of the nurse to break the visiting rules. Grateful, Jean popped her head out the door. "Thanks for allowing John to have communion," she told the nurse sitting at the desk. "The lay minister just left."

The nurse looked at her. "I've been sitting here for the last twenty-five minutes," she replied. "I didn't see anyone leave your room."

Puzzled, Jean approached a woman at the door of the

next room. "Did you see anyone coming out of our door-way?"

"No." The visitor shook her head. "And I've been standing here for at least a half hour."

Jean checked all the rooms on the floor, then went to the waiting rooms and reception hall. The gray lady had not registered at the desk. There *had* been a group of Catholic men bringing communion to the patients, but no woman of any age or description was among them. Exasperated, Jean gave up. It was peculiar, but best forgotten, especially since John seemed to suffer no ill effects.

John slept all day, and at four-thirty that afternoon he abruptly sat up in bed. Jean went cold with apprehension. Was he hallucinating again? But no. "Are the kids waiting in the foyer?" he asked her.

"Yes. Would you like me to get them?"

"No. I'll get dressed and walk down to visit with them."

"Absolutely not!" Jean gasped. "You're terribly sick—you'll be even worse after all that exertion...."

"I feel just fine, honestly," he told her.

Jean looked closer. John's waxen complexion had turned rosy; he looked better than he had in weeks. Relenting, she helped him into slippers and robe. The look of relief and joy on the children's faces when they saw him confirmed Jean's own suspicions. Her husband was going to get well.

The doctor examined John thoroughly the following morning and was completely mystified. "John's fever is gone, his eyes are clear, and he might as well go home as there isn't a sign of any illness," he told them. "I simply can't explain it." Jean saw no reason to mention the gray lady, not to a doctor of medicine. But John returned to normal activity within two weeks, and he has remained healthy to this day.

For a long time, Jean resisted the idea that their mysterious visitor had been an angel. Didn't angels appear in white shining robes, wearing gold halos? By contrast, her gray lady had been efficient, no-nonsense, detached, and completely in control of the situation. "She commanded firmly, prayed firmly, and after finishing her mission, vanished firmly," Jean says. "She was the most unangelic spirit I could ever imagine."

And yet...who could doubt the wondrous healing that had occurred? And hadn't there been comforting signs all along the way, evidence that she and John were not alone in this ordeal...hadn't she even heard that "second voice" reassuring her? "I think many people experience these special touches," Jean says, "but we're afraid others will ridicule us if we talk about them. But I was there, I saw the change in John, and now I consider life a loving gift."

Nor will Jean forget the fervent prayer she whispered during the crisis of illness. "Please, God, let him live...I need him...I love him...send me a miracle...."

God did—and a messenger to bring it.

# Rescue on the Tracks

*'Tis only when they spring to heaven that angels
Reveal themselves to you.*
ROBERT BROWNING, *PARACELSUS, PART V*

Carol Toussaint was driving her large station wagon across Arlington Heights, Illinois, about five P.M. one hot summer weekday. She was going to pick up one son from his guitar lesson, and her other youngsters, Dave and Katie, were in the backseat. It was past the time when she should have started dinner, and her mind was on getting home as soon as possible.

The traffic light was green. Carol turned left off the busy highway up a little incline and onto the railroad tracks that intersect the downtown area. But before she could complete her turn and travel through the railroad crossing, her engine suddenly died. She was stuck—blocking several lanes, with her front wheels resting in the track grooves.

Carol tried again and again to start the car, but the ignition wouldn't catch. The traffic light changed, cars began to honk, brakes screeched as rush-hour travelers attempted to go around her and avoid plowing into one another. Dave and Katie, hot, confined, and sensing their mother's distress, started to complain. It was a driver's worst nightmare.

Suddenly a young man wearing a white shirt and tie

loped casually over to Carol's open window. Dave, then only about five, thinks the man got out of a small brown car before approaching them.

"Did you know that you're in danger here?" the man asked softly, with an air of complete peace and tranquillity—in the midst of the rapidly snarling traffic.

"I sure am," Carol responded. "My husband's going to kill me for being late and not having dinner ready! If one of these drivers doesn't do it first...."

"No, I didn't mean that," the young man went on. "There's a train due through here in about half a minute. I'm going to have to move the car for you."

Carol had forgotten that at this time of day commuter trains whizzed through the crossing at frequent intervals. Some stopped, others didn't. And yes, now she noticed that there were several people standing at the station a block or two away. But even if this coming train was due to stop, it couldn't avoid hitting her—at this point it would still be traveling too fast!

Carol isn't sure what she did next—she was in such a panic that she can't remember. But she'll never forget the reaction of the serene young man. Nonchalantly he walked to the front of her car and gave it a little one-handed push. The huge station wagon dislodged easily from the track grooves, and as the crossing gates came down and warning bells began to clang, it rolled back across the tracks and safely over the little incline, where it again came to a stop.

Almost immediately, the train roared past. Stunned, Carol realized that, without the young man's help, her family would have been hit and killed. But where was he? The train had blocked her view for only a moment. How could he have disappeared in this open area without her seeing him?

By this time several passers-by and commuters were approaching Carol's car. "Need help, lady?" they asked. "Maybe we can push the car across the street to the gas station...."

How odd, Carol thought. No one was running or upset in any way. They all acted as if her car had stalled where it *now* was. No one seemed to realize that she and the children had just been rescued. Hadn't they witnessed her close call, or the young man?

But her children had. "Who was that guy who pushed us, Mom?" Dave asked from the backseat. "Where did he go?" If the man *had* arrived in a small brown car, it had somehow disappeared, even though traffic was snarled all around them.

"I have no idea, Dave," Carol said, puzzled. It was certainly a mystery. And it would take several days of musing before she began to realize just what had happened.

One commuter stood in the middle of the intersection and directed cars around the scene, while another went to alert the gas station. Mechanics and others pushed Carol's car down the rest of the incline to the station. Although the man in the white shirt had dislodged the large vehicle with one hand, it took eight people to move it all the way across the highway.

Carol's husband didn't get his dinner on time that night. He received a far greater gift.

# On a Wave of Light

*God heard the boy crying, and the angel of God called to Hagar from heaven and said to her, "What is the matter, Hagar? Do not be afraid; God has heard the boy crying as he lies there...."*

GENESIS 21:17

*In* 1949, Norma and Phil Smith (the names of everyone in this story have been changed) bought their first home. It was a two-family dwelling with a large unfinished attic. Although the Smiths had several children, they rented the unfinished second floor to the Taylors and their two children. Norma especially liked the daughter, Margaret. The families got along well, and the Taylor teens were thrilled to be godparents when Tommy Smith was born.

But something began to happen to Margaret. She dropped out of high school and stayed home all the time. In the spring of that year, when a priest at Norma's parish stopped by to discuss a situation with one of the Smith children, Norma told him about Margaret. "I'm concerned about her," she said. "She never goes out, and something seems to be wrong up there."

"Isn't Margaret's mother home?" the priest asked.

"No, she works at a department store," Norma told him. Only later did she recall that Mrs. Taylor was no longer em-

ployed. She had been let go because of "inappropriate behavior."

The priest went upstairs, but found nothing unusual.
Norma, busy with the demands of her large family, thought
no more about it.

Just a few months later, on June fourteenth, three-year-
old Tommy Smith disappeared. The four older Smith children were at school, and Norma and her two other preschoolers were at home. At that time, Norma was expecting
her eighth baby. When she couldn't find Tommy, she notified
the police.

Shortly afterward, a relative of the Taylors telephoned
and told Norma to go upstairs right away, that Tommy had
been seen entering the second-floor apartment. Using her
passkey, Norma admitted herself and found Tommy. He had
been drowned in the bathtub by Mrs. Taylor. The Smiths
realized too late that the Taylors were attempting to care for
their mentally ill mother alone. This was apparently why
Margaret had been sticking so close to home.

How does a person cope with a tragedy like this? How
does one survive? When Norma describes the desolation she
endured during the next several months, who among us can
comprehend her suffering? Reporters wrote of the murder in
detail. The Smith children, victims of their classmates' curiosity, were sent to various relatives to recover; most had
nightmares or developed other fears. Phil Smith, unable to
function at work, lost his job, turned to prescription drugs
to ease his emotional pain—and finally slipped into alcohol-
ism. Thirty-three-year-old Norma grieved.

"I wasn't debilitated," she says. "After all, there were six
children to care for as well as an unstable husband and an
expected baby. And the neighbors were very kind." But she

had fallen into a pit of sorrow from which there seemed no escape, and although the Taylors moved away, Norma was unable even to begin to heal. She began to believe she would grieve this way forever.

On November first, celebrated by Catholics as the Feast of All Saints, Norma attended an evening mass alone. She welcomed the unaccustomed solitude but, four weeks away from her due date, she was not only mentally bereft but also physically exhausted. Unbidden, her thoughts turned again to little Tommy. How very much she missed him! Why had this terrible thing happened, to the Taylor family as well as to them? Yes, she had prayed many times, and she knew God's strength was keeping her going. But how much longer would it sustain her? Right now, she felt as if she could not take another step.... *Oh, Tommy—I wish I knew you were all right*, she thought.

Suddenly a flash of blinding light illuminated the church's interior. Was it lightning? But no—almost as if the words were burned into her soul, Norma heard a message being flashed to her: *Mom, don't worry. Everything's going to be okay.*

"They weren't audible words. I didn't see anyone or hear a child's voice, but I knew that it was Tommy talking to me," Norma says. "It was almost like a blood transfusion, something that absolutely went into me and became a part of me. Instantly, I was ecstatically happy."

Through tears of joy, Norma looked around. Had others seen the brilliant flash? But people were behaving as usual, reading, praying, or looking preoccupied. No one had experienced anything out of the ordinary, and Norma was not surprised. Somehow she had known from the moment it happened that the words of consolation, the light, and the unbelievable rapture were meant only for her.

Outwardly, nothing had changed. Norma was still an uncomfortable pregnant mother. But during the following weeks she seemed to be steeped in bliss. Even after her husband found work and her new baby, Faith, was born healthy and happy, whenever she tried to tell family members of her experience, they suggested that she might have been hallucinating because of the traumas she had endured.

But Norma's life was never again the same. "I once asked an expert what the difference was between a hallucination and a vision. He told me that a vision leads to discovery and fulfillment. This has been my experience," she says. As years passed and she went through difficult times with her other children, she held on to the assurance that was given to her on All Saints' Day, the belief that her little son in heaven, perhaps through the power of an angel, had communicated a message of hope to her.

And she has been blessed by seeing her problems resolved, one by one. Everything, indeed, "has been okay."

# Winged Warriors

*An angel is a spiritual being, created by God without
a body, for the service of Christendom and the Church.*
MARTIN LUTHER, *TABLE TALK*

*T*he people of a small village had fervently prayed that
they would avoid bloodshed and injury perpetrated by war
raging in their country. But one night an army came to surround the village and capture it. The next morning, the people looked out, saw the gathering soldiers, and were terrified.
"We shall all be killed," they told one another in panic.

But one of their number, a young man who often led
evening prayers, seemed unconcerned. "We needn't be a-
fraid," he told his friends. "After all, our army is bigger than
theirs."

"But we don't have an army!" the villagers protested.

The young man prayed: "Lord, let their eyes be opened."

And suddenly the villagers saw *another* army—soldiers
everywhere upon the mountainside, poised for action and
glowing with a heavenly light.

The enemy soldiers apparently saw them too. Within
minutes, they had broken up and raced to safety. From that
point on, the villagers were left in peace.

This exciting story is from the Bible. It is related in the

Second Book of Kings (6:15–17). Many incidents like it have occurred in our times too, especially to missionaries.

Corrie ten Boom liked to recount a happening during the Jeunesse Rebellion in the Congo, when the rebels advanced on a school where two hundred children of missionaries lived. "They planned to kill both children and teachers," she writes. "In the school, they knew of the danger and therefore went to prayer. Their only protection was a fence and a couple of soldiers, while the enemy, who came closer and closer, amounted to several hundreds."

When the rebels were close by, suddenly something happened: They turned around and ran away! The same thing happened on the second and third day. One of the rebels was wounded and was brought to the missionary hospital. When the doctor was busy dressing his wounds, he asked him: "Why did you not break into the school as you planned?"

"We could not do it," the soldier said. "We saw hundreds of soldiers in white uniforms, and we became scared...."

"In Africa," Corrie explains, "soldiers never wear white uniforms. So it must have been angels. What a wonderful thing that the Lord can open the eyes of the enemy so that they see angels!" [16]

The Reverend John G. Paton was a missionary in the New Hebrides Islands in the Southwest Pacific. One night, hostile natives surrounded his headquarters, intent on burning out the Patons and killing them. John Paton and his wife, alone and defenseless, prayed all night that God would deliver them. When daylight came, they were amazed to see the attackers leave!

Eventually, the tribe's chief became a Christian, and Reverend Paton asked him what had kept the chief and his men from burning down the Patons' house that night.

The chief explained that he had seen many men standing guard—hundreds, in shining garments with drawn swords in their hands. They seemed to circle the mission station so that the natives were afraid to attack. Only then did John Paton realize that God had sent His angels to protect them.[17]

Another minister, attempting to reach families living in an obscure valley in Norway, had to descend a dangerous mountain trail. At one slippery and precipitous place he paused to pray for angelic assistance. Eventually, he reached the bottom safely.

At the first cottage, he met a couple who, he discovered, had been watching his treacherous journey down the mountain trail. "What has become of your companion?" was the couple's first question after greeting the missionary.

"What companion?" the missionary asked.

"The man who was with you."

"But no one was with me. I am traveling alone."

"Is that possible?" they exclaimed, surprised. "We were watching you as you came down, and we were positive that there were two of you crossing the mountain together."[18]

Sometime around 1950, missionaries named Egbert and Hattie Dyk went to work at Tseltal, an Indian village near Santo Domingo. All but one resident eventually became a Christian, but since there was much persecution from neighbors, the entire village packed up, walked for a day, and established a Christian community in the new place. The Dyks eventually left this settlement, but they heard about what transpired later from the missionary who took their place.

It seems that a man named Domingo Hernandez lived near this area and hated his Christian neighbors. He was determined to burn their settlement and slaughter all its inhabitants. Late one night he organized his fellow villagers, prepared pitch-pine torches and canoes and led them stealthily down the hill and across the river.

But before they had a chance to attack, they saw a bright light shining through the windows of every home in the Christian village. Then a strange luster shone over the entire area.

Domingo Hernandez and his men were so frightened that they turned and scrambled down the hill, plunged into the river, swam across, and ran, soaking wet, the half-mile to their homes.

The next morning, as the women from Hernandez's village were washing their clothes in the river, they called across to the Christian women on the other side. "What were those strange lights in your huts last night?" they asked.

"What lights?" the Christian women replied. "We had no lights burning. We were all asleep."

Finally, there is the story told by a pediatric nurse and member of an evangelical sisterhood who was serving in Danzig in 1945 after Russian troops had overrun many German towns. Local women were being abused, and nights were filled with terror. Nurses gathered as many women and children as they could and found temporary lodging in a small makeshift school. They often worked at night and, because of the lack of electricity, used candle stubs. Since theirs was the only lighted building, they, too, faced the danger of being invaded by the Russians. Yet the people called their building "the island of peace," because nothing bad ever seemed to happen there. Gradually, the stream of those seeking shelter increased.

One day a woman brought her children and begged the nurses to take them. The children had had a completely secular upbringing and had never seen anyone pray. That evening, as the community held a worship service, the new boy, instead of folding his hands with the rest, stared into the distance with wide eyes. The community sang a familiar song, asking God to send angels to "place golden weapons around our beds."

"When we said Amen, the boy came up to me and drew me out of the building," the nurse reported. "He kept tapping his breastbone and saying, 'Up to here. It came up to here on them.'"

The nurse asked him what he meant. Pointing to the gutter on the roof on the building, he repeated his statement. "The gutter came up to here on them!"

"What are you talking about?" the nurse asked.

The child told her that while everyone had been singing, he had seen a man ablaze with light at every corner of the building. The men were so tall that they towered above the roof.

"Now it was clear to me," the nurse noted, "why this house could be called 'the island of peace.'" [19]

# Companion Through the Storm

*Are not all angels ministering spirits sent to serve...?*
HEBREWS 1:14

*It* was two P.M. on a weekday in April 1974 in Louisville, Kentucky. Lynne Coates and her husband, Glynn, were enjoying an unexpected break from work, sitting on the steps of their porch. Their older sons were soon due home from school. Their youngest child, Collyn, would be at kindergarten at Southern Baptist Theological Seminary until about five.

The couple chatted comfortably for a while. Although the early-spring day was calm, small thin lines of clouds rippled across the sky.

Glynn frowned. "Look at the sky. The last time I saw one like that was when I was twelve, when a tornado hit."

Louisville was part of the Midwest's Tornado Alley, and the weather service routinely issued tornado warnings or watches, especially in spring. "I think we had all gotten a little blasé about tornados," Lynne admits now. "I certainly didn't expect to see one."

But she did. The sky got darker, the wind picked up, and Lynne began to feel apprehensive. The two older Coates boys came home, and as the tornado sirens began, Lynne made preparations to go into the basement. Glynn, however, hunted up his camera. "If I climb high enough," he told Lynne as he hoisted himself into the tree in their front yard, "I ought to be able to get some great pictures."

"Are you crazy?" Lynne screamed at him over the rapidly rising wind. "I just heard on the radio that Brandenburg has been leveled. Get into the basement! It's really happening!"

The family huddled together underground, listening to the roar that sounded like a train bearing down on the house, and later, the pounding rain. Everyone's thoughts centered on Collyn. Was he safe? Why hadn't they gone earlier to pick him up? But who could have guessed that this time there would be a real tornado?

In just minutes the storm had passed, and the family came out of the basement. Their neighborhood seemed relatively untouched, except for occasional debris and some downed power lines. "I'm going over to the seminary to get Collyn," Glynn announced, and left immediately. They would all feel better once their youngest child was with them.

Lynne gathered the older boys, and they gave thanks to God for bringing them through the storm. Then she found a portable radio and turned it on.

They listened to reports of the damage. And then they heard that the tornado had passed directly over the seminary. One of the buildings had lost its roof.

"Oh, Dear God, Collyn!" Lynne cried, and she flew to the telephone. She dialed the number of Collyn's kindergarten, but all she heard was the popping and crackling sounds that occur when a line is out of order. If the tornado had indeed gone in that direction, there must be a lot of damage, she realized. It was possible that telephone lines were down. But she had to know if Collyn was all right! And what was keeping Glynn? An ominous feeling settled within her heart. The seminary was only a fifteen-minute drive. Glynn should have been back before now.

Lynne couldn't have known that Glynn's route took him directly into the midst of the damage. What should have taken fifteen minutes would eventually be a two-hour trip, as he wended his way around uprooted trees, rescue vehicles, fallen wires, houses dumped helter-skelter, and, perhaps worst of all, people wandering the streets in a daze. The storm had virtually destroyed a three-thousand-acre park of old trees next to the seminary, and Glynn had to park many blocks from Collyn's building. There was no way to drive through the devastation.

At home, Lynne tried again and again to phone the seminary kindergarten, but the number wouldn't ring. Instead, she would hear clicks, then the phone would fall silent. She grew more and more distraught, and both children began to cry. *God, I can't stand any more of this*, she prayed. *You're the only one who can help us now. Please watch over Collyn and the other children, and keep them safe.*

Once more, Lynne tried to phone. After a few clicks, the phone suddenly started to ring! A calm, pleasant-sounding woman then picked it up. "Don't worry," she answered Lynne's frantic questions. "The children are fine. They were all taken to another building before the storm. Their teachers will stay with them as long as it takes the parents to pick them up."

Lynne hung up, and she and the boys shouted for joy. Collyn was safe! They would just have to wait.

More than two hours later, Glynn and Collyn arrived. Glynn told Lynne that he had found a sign posted on Collyn's building door, telling parents where to go to collect their children. He had gone to the building and found Collyn there safe. Collyn had no memory of the tornado at all, except for noticing a bent weather vane on top of one of the buildings.

Lynne accompanied Collyn to his classroom on his first day back to school. She wanted to get the name of the woman who had relieved her fear on the telephone. "I'd like to thank her," she explained to Collyn's teacher.

The teacher looked at Lynne in bewilderment. "But you couldn't have spoken with anyone," she said.

"Oh, but I did," Lynne assured her. "You can ask my older boys. I was frantic until this woman assured me that Collyn was fine."

"Mrs. Coates, that would have been impossible," the teacher insisted. "We put a sign on the door, locked the building, and moved the children before the tornado struck. There wasn't anyone here.

"And don't forget—our phone lines were destroyed. No call could have gotten through—or been answered."

Angels have been called our "companions in a storm." The Coates family knows, in a special way, what that lovely promise means.

# The Angels and the Padre

*Make yourself familiar with the angels, and behold them frequently in spirit; for without being seen, they are present with you.*

ST. FRANCIS DE SALES

*P*adre Pio, born in 1887 of simple farm people in Pietrelcina, Italy, was a monk who had the stigmata, the marks of Christ's crucifixion, etched in his hands, feet, and side, as did the founder of his order, St. Francis. Despite his own fragile health, he devoted his life to building homes for the sick, handicapped, and elderly.

Padre Pio had a particularly interesting relationship with angels. It is said that he "met" his own guardian angel as a youngster and occasionally received counsel from him; later, the two communicated in both prayerful and humorous dialogues. At times, according to witnesses, Padre Pio was able to read and speak languages he didn't know. When asked how he could do it, he said that his guardian angel translated for him. On occasion, a number of his fellow monks heard voices singing in heavenly harmony but couldn't discover the source of the music. Padre Pio explained that the voices were angels, escorting souls into heaven.

Padre Pio frequently sent his angel to someone who needed help. For example, Father Alessio Parente was assigned to assist the fragile monk from the chapel to his monastic cell every day. But Father Parente had a habit of oversleeping. Often he wouldn't hear his alarm clock or, half awake, he would switch it off. "Every time I overslept," he says, "I heard a voice in my sleep saying, 'Alessio, Alessio, come down!' and a knocking at my door. Realizing I was late, I would jump out of bed and run out into the corridor to see who called me, but there was nobody there. I would race down to the church and there I invariably found Padre Pio at the end of Mass giving the last blessing.

"One day I was sitting by Padre Pio's side, feeling ashamed at my lack of punctuality. I was trying to explain to him that I never seemed to hear the alarm, but he interrupted me. 'Yes, I understand you,' he said. 'But do you think I will continue to send my Guardian Angel every day to wake you? You'd better go and buy yourself a new clock.'

"It was only then that I realized who was knocking at my door and calling me in my sleep."

Padre Pio believed that people could send their angels to others to help or intercede. He encouraged his vast network of friends to send their angels to him if they could not come themselves. "Your angel can take a message from you to me," he would say, "and I will assist you as much as I can." On one occasion Cecil, an English friend of the Padre, was hurt in a car crash. A friend went to the post office to send a telegram to Padre Pio, requesting prayers for the accident victim. When the friend presented the telegram at the desk, the man gave him back a telegram from Padre Pio assuring him of his prayers for Cecil.

Later, after Cecil had recovered, he and his friend went to see Padre Pio. "How did you know of the accident?" both asked. "We got your telegram before we had sent ours."

"Do you think angels go as slowly as planes?" the monk responded, smiling.

On another occasion, an Italian girl, hearing of this saintly friar, sent her angel to ask for good health for her Uncle Fred. The girl then decided to visit Padre Pio for the first time. When she approached him, he joked with her: "Your angel kept me up all night, asking for a cure for your Uncle Fred!"

The mother of a desperately ill infant also sent the baby's angel to ask Padre Pio for prayers. As soon as she did so, she saw her tiny child shiver as if something had touched her. Although the doctors were mystified, the baby quickly improved and was sent home from the intensive-care unit.

"When speaking to people about these stories, the comments are often the same: 'Oh, well, Padre Pio was a very holy man, wasn't he?' or 'I'm just a poor sinner—why should an angel do anything to help me?," Father Parente says. "Yes, Padre Pio was a very holy man, but I believe our angels work well for each one of us too—if we only have faith."

When Padre Pio died on September 22, 1968, several American tourists in Italy saw angels in the night sky...angels who quietly disappeared as the sun rose.[20]

# Heavenly Directions

*Sweet souls around us watch us still,*
*Press nearer to our side;*
*Into our thoughts, into our prayers,*
*With gentle helpings glide.*

HARRIET BEECHER STOWE
*"THE OTHER WORLD"*

*A*ngels seem to be helpful in giving directions. Consider nineteen-year-old Charlotte, a student some years ago at Pacific Union College in Angwin, a small town about seventy-five miles north of San Francisco. Charlotte had a part-time job as housekeeper in a town some distance from campus. She traveled back and forth by bus, grateful for the income that made tuition and other expenses easier to meet.

One night, returning to Angwin tired and a bit careless, Charlotte boarded the wrong bus. It was too late to get off once she discovered what had happened. Eventually the big vehicle pulled into a busy terminal in San Francisco.

Charlotte was worried. She was not where she was supposed to be, and to make matters worse, she was surrounded late at night by strangers. Some sailors, recently returned from overseas, were leering at her. A drunk attempted to begin a conversation. She hurriedly walked away.

But where should she go? How would she find a bus to Angwin, that obscure little town, in this big building with its complex of tunnels? Unused to city life, Charlotte looked for someone to help her, but there was not another woman on the platform where the buses were loading. No policeman was in sight. The information booth bore a sign: CLOSED FOR THE NIGHT. There were only strange men to be seen, derelicts moving about in the shadows.

Then it came to her. The college's dean of women had made sure all the students memorized Psalm 34: "The angel of the Lord encamps around those who fear him, and delivers them."

"You never know," the dean said, "when you might need it."

Quickly Charlotte found a ladies' room, went in, locked the door behind her, and fell to her knees. *Dear God*, she prayed, *I'm lost and afraid. Please help me find my way home. According to your Holy Word, deliver me. Amen.*

Charlotte opened the door and stepped into the main area of the terminal again. Just then a young man passed in front of her. She noticed immediately that he was carrying what appeared to be a large black Bible.

*A Bible!* Charlotte thought. *Maybe he's one of the Pacific Union students returning to school!* In any event, she decided to follow him. Surely a man with a Bible would be trustworthy.

He led her through several long corridors, took an underpass to another part of the terminal, and hurried up a flight of stairs from a dimly lit concourse to a remote loading platform. Never could Charlotte have discovered this circuitous route by herself, she realized. Then all at once, there it was—a bus with big letters on the front that spelled ANGWIN! And it was about to pull out. The last one out of San Francisco that night. How fortunate for her!

Still close behind him, Charlotte followed the young man onto the bus. Only one seat remained, and he turned his back to her, as if to speak to the bus driver, and allowed her to pass him to the seat. Charlotte sank down, her eyes still on the stranger, relieved and grateful, and somewhat amazed ...for the driver did not seem to see the young man at all!

In a moment, the young man turned and got off the bus. No one was paying any attention to him. Only Charlotte watched through the window, her eyes following the young man for a few feet when, although he was in clear sight, he simply vanished. *Like a light going out,* Charlotte thought.

As the bus driver closed the door and the big vehicle pulled out of the station, Charlotte shot a heartfelt prayer of thanks to heaven. The Word of God does not fail, she knew. She had been delivered by an angel of the Lord.[21]

Bus trips and collegians played a part in Suzanne's experience too. It was a typical Minnesota winter, snowy and freezing. Suzanne's seven-year-old daughter, Jennifer (not their real names), needed to visit a specialist in downtown Minneapolis. Suzanne never felt comfortable driving on slick streets, and there already had been several substantial snowfalls, so she had decided to use the Metro system for the first time. "I was apprehensive, and I prayed that I would know where to go," she says. "My daughter was already nervous and didn't want to see another doctor. It was cold—I just wanted the day to go smoothly."

When Suzanne and Jennifer reached the bus stop, there was one rider waiting, a cheerful girl of about eighteen.

Suzanne smiled at her and asked, "By any chance, would you be going downtown?"

"Yes, I'm going to class at the University of Minnesota,"

the young woman told her. Suzanne had thought the university was in a completely different area, but, admittedly, her sense of direction was doubtful. "I'm from a small town just south of here," the girl explained. "I got a ride to the bus stop today from a friend."

Suzanne warmed to the girl's friendliness, while noticing that she seemed shabbily dressed. "Her heavy overcoat was really out of date, and I remember thinking that I hoped someday she'd have a good enough job to buy better clothes if she wanted them," Suzanne recalls. "I told her about our journey, and my concern about getting us there."

Without hesitation, the girl explained bus protocol—having proper change, pulling the cord a block from where Suzanne wanted to stop, and then she added, "Actually, since I'm going near there, why don't I just ride with you and make sure you find the right building?"

"Oh, I couldn't let you do that," Suzanne protested. "Wouldn't the trip be out of your way?" *Surely* the university couldn't be this way....

"It's no problem," the young woman assured her.

The bus came, the trio boarded and chatted comfortably on the way downtown. Suzanne was feeling more relaxed, less guilty about accepting her companion's help. She would certainly do the same for a stranded stranger, so it didn't seem all that unusual. But she *had* been quite fortunate to meet this charming young person.

The three got off the bus at the proper stop and walked toward the Nicollet Mall, about two blocks away. Suzanne knew the address of the Medical Arts Building, but it was hard locating street numbers on the structures. They had unknowingly walked past their destination, crossed half a street, and were on a pedestrian safety walk when Suzanne realized that the buildings on the other side were too small to be what they wanted.

Suzanne glanced back. "Look!" she said. "We just passed it. There it is—see the name carved into its side?"

The girl laughed. "It sure is!"

Suzanne and Jennifer turned back toward the building, while their companion continued on in the same direction. Just a second or two passed before Suzanne realized the girl was leaving them, and she turned to thank her.

Traffic was sparse and few pedestrians were out on this cold day, but their cheerful companion had completely disappeared. "My last view of her," Suzanne recalls, "was with her arm raised as if in farewell, as though, even before Jennifer and I turned to look at the Medical Arts Building, she knew we had found our destination."

Later, Suzanne discovered that the University of Minnesota campus wasn't anywhere near downtown Minneapolis. Nor would a student get there via the route they took.

But as Suzanne realized, the "student" had a different destination all along.

# "Like Touching God"

*What he did see was light: light from the Heavenly
Host as they swept the sky clean from one end to the
other...*
FRANK PARETTI, *THIS PRESENT DARKNESS*

"Angels have been a positive and visible presence in my
life as long as I can remember; I am unafraid and secure
when they are around," Fran Hamilton wrote to me. "I have
learned to distinguish their presence by a certain feeling. It
is not euphoria or elation or wild heart-pounding. It's security, serenity. It's 'all's right with the world.' It's like touching your God."

Fran has had several experiences with angels. Once she
attended the same morning mass as her son's school class. It
was announced that one of the children would be making his
first communion. Mass began, and all seemed normal. Then
about midpoint, Fran saw lights coming into the sanctuary
area from all directions. "They appeared as small, but extremely bright, little balls," Fran says. "There were so many
and they created a glow so intense that I had to shut my
eyes. Apparently no one else in church saw them, but I believed they were holy presences, coming to share and be a
part of this child's first-time communion."

The brilliance continued as Fran and the rest of the congregation approached the altar. Then the lights danced and

sparkled and gradually merged, creating a radiance so blazing that Fran again had to close her eyes. After receiving communion, she found herself back in her pew—with no memory of how she got there. When she opened her eyes after her communion prayer, the light had gone.

Fran has been unable to trace this child, now an adult, but she thinks there was probably something significant about him. She is sure that, one day, she will understand why so many angels attended his first communion.

Late one night Fran and her husband, Bob, were driving south on I–71 to their home in Columbus, Ohio, after a meeting when they realized they had a flat tire. Too late, they recalled that the spare was also flat.

"My husband decided to drive on the berm to the freeway exit, in hope that an all-night filling station was nearby," Fran explains. "While he inched along, I began praying to my guardian angel. The farther we went, the more evident it became that there was no filling station anywhere. My prayers became more focused, until we reached a parking area of a small closed grocery store and stopped under the overhead lights. I became very calm and suspected that I had no more need to pray."

Within moments, a small foreign car pulled up, and an attractive woman got out and casually walked up to their car. "She was probably in her late twenties, tall, slim, with long brown hair," Fran says. She seemed unusually serene and calm.

"Are you folks in trouble?" she asked through the window. "Can I do anything to help?"

"I need air in my spare tire," Bob explained.

"I can drive you to Grove City, about two miles down the

road," the young woman offered. "There's an all-night filling station there."

"That would be wonderful," Bob said.

Fran decided to wait in the car. She wasn't nervous at being left alone, but gradually she began replaying the incident in her mind. Why would a young woman stop on a deserted street at night to help two strangers? And that unusual aura of security and peace around her.... Fran felt peaceful too, in the familiar way that always graced her when angels were especially near.

Soon Bob and the young woman arrived with the air-filled spare. Bob started to replace the tire, and the woman said good-bye and left. "Did she tell you her name?" Fran asked as she and her husband finally drove toward home.

"She told me she was the wife of the manager of the Rax Restaurant in Grove City," Bob said. "Tomorrow, first thing, I'm going to go to the restaurant and thank her again."

"You won't find her there," Fran told him. "She's not married to the manager—or to anyone else, for that matter. She was an angel."

"Oh, for heaven's sake!" Bob scoffed at Fran's prediction.

The next morning, he went to the restaurant. Soon he was back, amazed. "The manager has no wife," he told Fran. "When I described her—and insisted that she had helped us—he looked at me like he was questioning my sanity."

Bob and Fran never had the chance to thank their rescuer again. But Fran thinks the lady knows how grateful they are.

# The Boy Who Drowned

*"See that you do not look down on one of these little
ones. For I tell you that their angels in heaven always
see the face of my Father in heaven...."*

MATTHEW 18:10

It was April 1981, and the Hardy family of Palestine, Texas,
was enjoying a visit with their cousins in Houston. The house
had a backyard pool, and three-year-old Jason Hardy had
been cautioned by everyone to stay in the front yard, away
from the pool.

Soon, however, Sue Hardy realized that her little boy was
not where he was supposed to be. She ran immediately to
the pool, but its surface was undisturbed. "I thought Jason
couldn't have fallen in, because he would be floating on top,"
Sue says. "I didn't know then that drowning victims sink to
the bottom." Sue ran back to the front yard, down the street,
then into the house, her concern mounting by the minute.

Finally, following an instinct, she and her niece returned
to the pool—and this time Sue saw something on the bottom.
Her niece jumped in and brought Jason to the surface. "My
world turned upside down when she handed me my dead
baby," Sue says. "He had no pulse, no heartbeat, and was
turning black." Clutching her child's limp body, Sue
screamed in anguish. Then she began to pray.

The family called the paramedics, and when they arrived Sue went upstairs. "I phoned an elder from my church in Palestine," she says, "and I told him we needed a miracle right now. Jason had been without a heartbeat for almost an hour, but I knew God could do anything He decided to do." After the phone call Sue lay down on the floor of the bedroom and prayed. "Jesus, Jesus," was all she could find the strength to say.

A few minutes later, one of Sue's daughters came to tell her that the paramedics had gotten Jason's heart started again. "Immediately, I was filled with peace," Sue relates. "I had Jason when I was forty-one, after my three older children were almost grown up. Somehow I knew that God had not given me this late blessing only to have him taken away."

Herman Hospital sent its Life Flight helicopter to take Jason to intensive care. By the time Sue drove there, doctors were painting a bleak picture. "They said that when a brain is deprived of oxygen for three to six minutes, damage begins," she explains. Jason had been clinically dead when he arrived at the hospital, and doctors felt that if he survived, he would be paralyzed and profoundly brain damaged.

"No. You watch and see," Sue told them. "Jason will walk out of this hospital by himself."

The physicians looked at one another. Obviously this little boy's mother couldn't yet absorb what had happened. They decided not to explain any more of the terrible consequences she faced.

Jason, in a coma and still considered clinically dead, was placed on a life-support system. On the fifth night he developed pneumonia, and hospital personnel felt the end was near. Clinging to the peace she had experienced in the bedroom, Sue phoned elders from a local church in Houston and asked them to visit her son. They did and anointed him as Sue and her family waited in the hall.

"Mrs. Hardy?" One of the elders came to the door. "Your little boy's eyes are fluttering." The three-year-old had just wet the bed. His brain was apparently waking up!

Not only did Jason walk out of the hospital twenty days later, he soon began to talk. Seven months after his terrible accident, his physician pronounced him healthy. Today, Jason is an active handsome boy, completely normal in every way. Sue gives thanks to God every day for His awesome miracle. And maybe for some extra protection as well. . . .

Being only three, Jason was far too young to talk about why he went to the pool and how he happened to fall in. As years passed, Sue assumed that he remembered nothing except what his family had told him about his accident and hospitalization. One night when Jason was about six or seven, however, he was watching a television show when a shot of a swimming pool came into view. "It was dark underneath that pool," Jason suddenly said.

Sue was immediately alert. Was he remembering something about his accident? "Tell me about it," she said.

"It was dark," the little boy repeated, "but the angel stayed with me."

"The angel, Jason?"

"Uh-huh. He was there so I wouldn't be afraid."

That is all Jason has ever said about his miraculous rescue. But to his family, it is enough.

# Watcher in the Woods

*The very presence of an angel is a communication.*
*Even when an angel crosses our path in silence, God*
*has said to us, "I am here. I am present in your life."*
TOBIAS PALMER, *AN ANGEL IN MY HOUSE*

Saint John Bosco, as tradition has it, was often bothered by toughs who threatened to mug him as he passed them on his mission to serve the poor. Eventually, a large fierce-looking black dog began to appear alongside John and to accompany him through the danger zones. When John reached a place of safety, the dog would vanish. Perhaps guardian angels are not *always* disguised as people....

Barbara Johnson had completed her general-nursing training at the Royal Adelaide Hospital in Australia. She worked six months in Melbourne, then went to Sydney to train as a midwife at St. Margaret's Hospital.

Barbara's brother and his wife lived in a suburb of Sydney, so on her first day off, she took the train to their home for a visit. Everyone had a lovely day, and Barbara left about nine P.M. for the return journey.

"I was feeling proud," she admits. "Although I later got to know the underground subway system well, this was my first time traveling beneath the city. Yet I had found my way around and gotten off at the right stop." Confidently, she climbed up to a well-lit street and decided to take a shortcut through a park.

Barbara wasn't apprehensive as she began her walk. "I had walked in cities at night, and had learned that you keep your pace brisk but not hurried, so onlookers don't think you're afraid." She moved purposefully down the path, and it was only after a few moments that she realized the park was extremely dark inside, and Oxford Street—and the hospital—was much farther than she had anticipated.

There was no one else in the park, at least no one she could see. But Barbara had the feeling she was being watched. From time to time she saw a glow, like the end of a lit cigarette, in the shadows. Her heart began to pound. Was she in danger? If someone grabbed her and pulled her into the bushes here, there would be little she could do to protect herself. But if she bolted, she could lose her way in the darkness or fall and hurt herself.

There was no choice but to keep going. Barbara quickened her pace and stared straight ahead, fixing her eyes on that distant glow, the streetlights that signaled safety....

She was about halfway through the park when she sensed movement to her right. Oh, no! As if everything wasn't frightening enough, there was a large white Alsatian dog right next to her.

"This breed was very intimidating, because the police used them as guard dogs," Barbara says. "They were known to be vicious." Frantically, she looked around for the dog's owner, but the park was deserted. What would she do if the dog charged her? Barbara pictured herself lying bleeding on the dirt, vulnerable to attacks from both man and beast. Her heart raced even faster.

Curiously, the dog seemed anything *but* bad-tempered. It

simply trotted alongside her as if it belonged. Barbara slackened her pace, hoping the furry monster would pass her, but the dog slowed as well. Then she stopped. "Go away, dog." Timidly she tried to shoo it. "Go away, now!"

But the dog stopped too, as if rooted to the spot, and looked up at her. Its demeanor didn't change, nor was it agitated or responsive. It simply *stayed*, like an obedient guard assigned to her side.

Barbara saw no other option but to keep moving, and that's just what she did, almost breaking into a run as she reached the welcome lights of Oxford Street. The dog stood beside her as she glanced down the street to check the traffic. Was it going to follow her across?

But just as she stepped off the curb, Barbara looked to her right once more. The dog was gone.

Relieved, Barbara hurried to the hospital dorm and made herself a cup of tea in the kitchenette. "You look exhausted," one of the nurses said.

"I've had a traumatic experience," Barbara explained. "I took a shortcut just now through the park—"

"You went into the park at night?" another nurse interrupted. "Oh, you're new, you wouldn't have known. But many crimes take place in that park!"

Aghast that she had ventured into such a dangerous and poorly lit area after dark, the two nurses related one horror story after another, and Barbara thought back with consternation to the cigarette glow in the shadows. Oh, what might have happened to her! God must have been watching over her....

"And suddenly I was filled with a sense of guardian angels, and I knew without question that the dog had been mine," Barbara says. "There was just no other explanation for his arrival, his behavior, and his sudden disappearance. I felt grateful that God chose to take such personal care of me, and that He was always ready to protect us, even from our own foolishness."

Barbara eventually worked in New Guinea, where she met her American husband. Later she accompanied him to Wisconsin, where the family now lives. She never saw her angel again, but she has named him Guiseppe and feels a bond that has endured through the years.

# The Quiet Protectors

*The Angels keep their ancient places*
*Turn but a stone and start a wing!*
*'Tis ye, 'tis your estrangéd faces*
*That miss the many splendored thing.*
FRANCIS THOMPSON
*"THE KINGDOM OF GOD"*

*I*mpulses. Aren't they just intuition? Sometimes. But the following stories suggest something more specific at work.

As a traveling businessman, Frank was often away from home for the whole week, returning only on Saturday. Many times he sent his guardian angel to watch over his young family in his absence.

One Friday afternoon about five, Frank had an overpowering feeling that something was wrong at home. *Guardian angel, go to my family and protect them*, he prayed. The apprehension immediately left him.

The next day Frank arrived home. "How was everything while I was gone?" he asked his wife, still remembering that strange ominous moment.

"Oh, Frank, we almost had a tragedy!" his wife burst out. She'd taken her eyes off Timmy, their four-year-old, for only a few seconds, and the child had run out into the street. At that very moment a car was speeding along the lane toward him. Horrified, Frank's wife saw that she could never reach her son in time.

But when the car was about thirty feet away, the driver saw the child and braked, with such force that the car turned around in a complete circle twice, then came to rest directly in front of Timmy, who had been frozen to the spot in terror. The driver, instead of giving vent to anger, leaped from the car and shouted, "It's a miracle! A miracle that I was able to stop in time!"

"What time did this happen?" a shaken Frank asked.

"Yesterday," his wife answered. "Just at five o'clock."

Sister Martha had a similar experience. She was on night duty in a hospital and had to go to the cellar to fetch some medicine from the walk-in freezer. As she was searching the shelves, the door closed unexpectedly behind her.

"Oh, no!" Sister Martha murmured in dismay. The freezer had no interior security handle, and she was locked in.

At that late hour, it was useless to call, for no one would hear her. So instead, Sister Martha began to beseech the angels to help her. "I was mainly concerned because the patients in my ward would be unattended all night," she says today. "My own danger—death by freezing—had not yet registered in my mind."

Just a short time passed and Sister Martha heard something on the other side of the door. Before she could call out, the handle turned and the door swung open. On the other side was one of the nursing sisters.

The women stared at each other, astonished. Sister Martha was amazed that her prayer had been answered so swiftly. But her companion was even more dumbfounded.

"I had gone to bed," the other nun explained, "but I kept

feeling that I was supposed to go down to the cellar and make sure everything was in order." She tried to ignore the prod, but finally, when it would not go away, she gave in. "I just opened the freezer door for a last check," she told Sister Martha. "I had no idea anyone was locked in."

Andrew Smith had been hunting in a wooded, undeveloped pocket of Jefferson County, Missouri, about thirty-five miles southwest of St. Louis, with a friend, Joe (not their real names). It was a dreary, chilly day in late autumn.

Andrew is very much an outdoorsman, thoroughly grounded in safety procedures. He would never carelessly handle a gun or permit anyone else to do so. He had never hunted with Joe before, although the two men sometimes fished together.

"There are several 'givens' in firearms handling," Andrew explains. "A gun is never pointed at anything other than what one wishes to shoot. When two hunters walk side by side, with guns cradled, each points his muzzle in the direction away from the other. When one is walking with a loaded gun, the safety is engaged to prevent accidental discharge. One does not walk with a finger on the gun's trigger. When hunting or otherwise carrying firearms, one must be constantly alert to positions and movements of others in relation to oneself." These rules were second nature to Andrew and, he assumed, to Joe.

The two men had hunted the periphery of a plot of small fields and thick woodland, and they were walking back to the car up a rough road. Joe was on Andrew's right with his gun properly cradled and pointing away from Andrew.

"An ingrained awareness about safety factors was probably what alerted me that Joe had changed position in some subtle way," Andrew recalls. "I glanced to my right and saw that Joe's gun was now cradled on the wrong side, with the muzzle pointing toward my head. I was about to ask him to change the gun back to its proper place. Under normal circumstances, that's what I would have done."

Instead, Andrew heard a voice inside his head. It was not a familiar voice, and he knew immediately that it was not audible, because Joe didn't look up or react to the sound. And yet it was as loud and as clear—and as infused into his consciousness—as if the speaker had been standing on Andrew's left side.

And perhaps the speaker was. For he said, "Andrew! Take two quick steps forward."

Andrew does not ordinarily respond to orders without question. But he obeyed instantly. He had just taken the second step when Joe's shotgun discharged into the space he had occupied.

The two men stood dazed at the near miss. "What happened?" Andrew, shaken, demanded.

"I don't know." Joe shook his head, appalled.

"Didn't you have the safety engaged?"

"I *thought* so. And my finger certainly wasn't on the trigger."

"It must have been. And why was the gun pointing at me?"

Joe had no answer. He was bewildered and ashamed at what appeared to be three unconscious violations of safety rules. How could such a thing have happened? The men were never able to reach a satisfactory explanation.

"On many occasions I have realized that I was in dangerous situations," Andrew reflects. "Sometimes I have failed to react quickly enough, resulting in an injury of one sort or another. And I've never had any indication that I'm exempt from the consequences of my own carelessness or attention lapses.

"But could it be only chance that I had a sudden once-in-a-lifetime compulsion to move away from a gun?" Ordinarily Andrew is able to find natural explanations for unusual happenings. But this event exceeds the limits of coincidence. He has concluded that it was direct intervention, on his behalf, by his guardian angel.

In none of the above or similar episodes that people shared with me, did participants *see* benevolent beings. "It would be hard—yes, impossible—to 'prove' that anything supernatural was at work," one wrote. "But do I believe that I was touched and protected? Yes, oh a thousand times, yes!"

# Silent Circle

*Around our pillows, golden ladders rise,*
*And up and down the skies,*
*With winged sandals shod,*
*The angels come and go, the messengers of God!*
R. H. STODDARD, *"HYMN TO THE BEAUTIFUL"*

$\mathscr{V}$iola Rockett had always been a responsible person, graduating from her small high school in Charleston, Mississippi, in three years with a ninety-five percent average. Falling in love and marrying at nineteen was a challenge, but she handled her new responsibilities with her usual maturity and common sense. "I've never been easily scared or suspicious," she explains. "I came to know God when I was thirteen and always had a pretty firm faith after that."

Life with her young husband, A.J., wasn't easy, however. It was tough to find work in their part of Mississippi. Two little daughters were born during those years, straining their budget even more.

When Viola was twenty-five, the couple moved to Mathiston, Mississippi, a small town with just a few stores and a post office. A.J. had been repairing and selling used cars to support his family, so he rented an old repair and body shop, filled with stripped-down autos, tools, and junk—an easy structure to break into, if there had been anything worth stealing.

A room that had once been the auto-parts store connected to the body shop. "Two of the walls were made of ceiling-to-floor glass—like showroom windows—with ceiling-to-floor shades," Viola describes it. "The only light bulb hung in the kitchen area, with a string to pull it on and off." Here, in this room, the family lived.

Viola had never known such isolation. A.J. was gone several nights a week, buying and selling cars, and she was without a phone, cut off from a support system of family and friends. Viola tried hard to be brave, but at night the room was especially scary. She felt vulnerable with those long windows in front of her, even though the shades were pulled down. It was common knowledge in the town that she was often alone at night. What would she do if anyone tried to break in? How could she protect herself and her daughters?

One night, alone with the girls, Viola awakened in a dreadful mindless fear. She had not been having a nightmare. In fact, there seemed no reason for the terror that had abruptly gripped her, but she sensed great danger all around her. "I was so frightened that I believed that someone or something was actually *in* the room with us," she says, "and I knew that I would have to find the courage to get out of bed, make my way across the floor, find the string hanging from the bulb, and turn on the light."

Anyone who has suffered from an anxiety attack will know how difficult it was for Viola to move. Her heart pounding, more terrified than she had ever been in her life, she managed to stumble across the floor and find the string. But when she turned on the light and looked around, nothing seemed to be wrong. The bleak room looked just the same.

And yet instead of relief, the fear came again, an unbelievable wave, and Viola was convinced that the peril was now actually right outside those covered windows, so close she could almost touch it. If she ran outside to get help, she would plunge right into whatever was there. But if she stayed inside, there was little chance of keeping an intruder out, not with the building's flimsy, run-down construction. Not knowing what else to do, Viola knelt in the middle of the dreary setting. "God, help us," she cried out. "Thank You for Your love and care. Please keep us safe now."

She looked up. Suddenly, although the shades had been down, she saw them dissolve from the windows. And on the outside of each of those ten or twelve panes of glass, she saw a huge figure slowly descend and fold his wings to his side. "Nothing seemed like a dream or slow motion. It was all very normal," she says. Except—they were angels!

Facing outward with their backs to her, these wondrous beings were so tall that their heads were above the tops of the windows and she could not see them. But she could see the wings folding behind their bodies as each figure slowly got into position. A phalanx of heavenly guards, sent to protect her in answer to her plea. How much God must love her! It was unbelievable.

The vision lasted only a few minutes. As Viola's stunned eyes traveled from one silent figure to another, the shades suddenly reappeared and once again covered the glass. Viola and her daughters were alone in the room. And yet, she knew that they would never be alone.

Viola never discovered what was threatening her and the children that night. But she doesn't remember being afraid often in the thirty-some years that have passed. "God gave me the grace to see what is real, that He never abandons us," Viola says. His touching gift has sustained her ever since.

# A Smiling Child

*With silence only as their benediction*
*God's angels come*
*Where, in the shadow of a great affliction,*
*The soul sits dumb.*

JOHN GREENLEAF WHITTIER
*"TO MY FRIEND ON THE DEATH OF HIS SISTER"*

*G*retchen and her husband, Fred, had had a long and happy marriage, but Fred had recently died. And although Gretchen had a son and four grandchildren who loved her very much, one does not easily recover from such a momentous loss.

During the first few months, Gretchen had been numb with grief and unable to weep. But she had progressed beyond the initial shock stage, and now, it seemed, crying was all she did. "I was beginning to dread meeting anyone," she recalls, "because I was so afraid that I would burst into tears in the middle of an ordinary conversation." People had been very kind, but Gretchen didn't want anyone pitying her and she didn't want her sorrow to make others uncomfortable.

On this Sunday, Gretchen went to church by herself and selected an empty pew. She saw no familiar faces, and she was relieved. At least if her anguish threatened to overwhelm her, she could slip out quietly.

As she sat in the pew, she thought again of Fred, and

desolation and grief swept in waves across her spirit. "I could hardly keep from crying out," she says. It was hard to endure such continuous mourning. Would it ever end? In another moment, she was going to weep....

Suddenly, a small boy entered the pew and sat next to Gretchen. She eyed him through her tears. He had light-brown hair, was neatly dressed in a little brown suit, and appeared to be about six years old. And he was looking up at her in the most familiar way, smiling as if he knew her.

It was peculiar. Children rarely attended church alone in this particular congregation, especially at such an early hour. Where could his family be? Even stranger was the fact that, although the youngster had picked up the church prayer book to read, he kept edging toward Gretchen. "He moved nearer and nearer, very casually. He would read, then look up, catch my eye, and beam. His whole attitude made it clear that he had come to keep me company." What a darling child!

As the little boy snuggled close to Gretchen, something else began to happen. She felt her heart lighten. Somehow, although she hadn't believed such a thing would ever happen again, she began to feel, yes, happy. It was only a fleeting emotion, like a brief little kiss, but she felt it.

And she would be happy again. She knew it now without question. "A time to mourn and a time to dance...." Gretchen was still very much in mourning, but the love and sweetness in the little boy's face had given her a glimpse of a better time yet to come.

But who was this child? Gretchen looked down at him, and again he smiled at her in that intimate and penetrating manner. She *must* know him ... why else would he be behaving this way? Of course. He was probably the son of a younger neighbor or friend who, aware of Gretchen's loss and seeing her sitting alone, had sent her little boy up to share the pew. Gretchen would have to thank his parents for their thoughtfulness. She would watch where the child went after the service.

As the service ended, Gretchen and the boy left the pew and headed for the front door. There were people around, but not a huge crowd, and the child was right next to Gretchen. "What is your name?" she asked him. "Do I know your mother?"

But instead of answering, he looked up at her for one last smile. And then, as Gretchen's eyes scanned the crowd to find someone searching for him, the child vanished. He was there—and then he simply wasn't. Gretchen didn't see him go, but when she glanced down, the spot next to her was vacant.

"I kept looking for him among the people until everyone had left, but I never saw him again, nor did I meet anyone who knew him or had sent him."

But after that Sunday, Gretchen never felt quite so alone again. Gradually the truth seemed to come upon her—that an ordinary child, no matter how charming, would not have been able to lift her spirits in that mysterious and welcome way. Instead, the child had been sent by Someone Who understood her suffering and was reaching out to comfort and heal her.

# The Boy in the Blue Suit

*Was there no star that could be sent...*
*to heal that only child?*
EMERSON, *"THRENODY"*

*M*ichael Sullivan of Howard Beach, New York, is the author of *Joy to My Youth*, a yet-unpublished memoir of a happy boyhood in the 1920s. When he heard about my angel project, he generously offered to let me retell and share with readers the following experience from his book:

Michael awakened feverish and queasy on the morning of his confirmation day in 1925. But he couldn't miss this major event! Saint Bartholomew's parish in Elmhurst was part of the Brooklyn diocese and, in those days, the bishop confirmed there once every four years. If Michael had to stay home today, he wouldn't be able to receive the sacrament until he was fourteen.

Reluctantly Michael's father decided he could go, and his older sister, Mary, helped the ten-year-old dress and walked him to the church. She wouldn't be able to stay because there were so many children to be confirmed that the church couldn't accommodate any family or well-wishers.

Michael lined up with the others, slowly marched into church, and took his assigned place in the pew, just as he had practiced. The bishop, wearing gold vestments and a huge gold miter, sat on a special chair at the center of the altar, surrounded by priests. It was an impressive sight.

The organ played. Finally the boys in Michael's pew filed out and walked up the aisle. "I was glad I had only a short distance to go," he says, "because my knees wobbled."

Gently, the bishop touched Michael's cheek and uttered the words of the sacrament. Then Michael returned to his pew to kneel up straight, as he had been instructed. But he ached all over ... and there was such a long line of boys still approaching the altar.... The candlelight seemed to blur, and the bishop was blurred too.... Michael fainted and fell into the center aisle.

When Michael came to, he was sitting in an oak chair in the sacristy, a small room behind the altar. The pastor, who had been waving smelling salts under his nose, looked relieved. "You'll be all right now," he said. "Just sit here and rest awhile."

A window was open and a soft April breeze filtered into the sacristy. The pastor returned to the ceremony, leaving Michael with the usher who had carried him out. "Are you feeling better?" the usher asked after some time had passed.

Michael nodded. "I guess so."

"You don't have to wait until the ceremony's over," the usher pointed out. "Do you think you can walk home?"

Michael thought he could. Quietly he slipped out a side door and walked cautiously down an alley and across the street to a path that cut diagonally through an empty lot. He was familiar with this trail—he took it every day to school.

But today the path seemed like a long, winding road. Every step was an effort, and Michael's body started to ache again, just as it had when he had tried to kneel up straight in church. "I recalled Sister's instructions that the Holy

Spirit would come upon you in the Sacrament of Confirmation and give you strength," Michael says. "This thought had a calming effect, and I managed to get halfway before I knew I wasn't going to make it to the end of the path."

He turned and looked back at Saint Bartholomew's, hoping that the ceremony had ended and friends would come out and find him. But there was no one anywhere. He began to feel light-headed and weak, exactly as he had felt just before his faint. In desperation, he looked around for a rock to sit on, or a clean patch of grass on which to lie.

Just then—although there had been no one in view—a boy in a blue suit appeared beside him. He was older and taller than Michael, but he had a friendly face. Michael was glad to see him. "Were you just confirmed?" he asked.

"No," the boy said with a smile. Strength seemed to emanate from him, and Michael's queasiness passed. The boy started to walk up the path, and automatically Michael took his place beside him. The path didn't seem so long now.

The boy spoke with animation, and they discussed many topics. "My head was still fuzzy and I couldn't quite place him, but he undoubtedly knew me, all about me," Michael says. "He knew that my mother wasn't living. He knew my two sisters, and that my dad was a wonderful man."

As they left the lot and walked up Lamont Avenue, Michael told the boy about the previous highlight of his life. His dad had taken him to the second game of the World Series in 1923. Babe Ruth had hit two home runs, and the Yankees had beaten the Giants, four to two.

The boy listened, and he seemed to know all about it. He knew that John McGraw had taken out his starting pitcher, Hughie McQuillan, and had put in Jack Bentley. He knew that Irish Meusel, Yankee Bob Meusel's brother, had hit a home run for the Giants.

The sun filtered through the maple trees in full bud. There was something about the sun, the spring-green trees, and the warm companionship of this boy that made Michael feel stronger with every step. They reached the corner. "You've only got one more block to go," the boy said, looking toward the white gabled house in the distance.

"That's right," Michael said, studying his companion's face for the first time. The boy's eyes shone. He walked across the street in the other direction, turned, smiled, and waved at Michael. As he waved, a shimmering light outlined his body.

A delivery truck came between the two. Michael waited for the truck to pass so that he could wave back at the boy. The truck passed. The boy in the blue suit was nowhere in sight.

Michael ran the remaining block home, and dared not tell anyone about his companion. During the next few days he searched the neighborhood, but he never saw the boy in the blue suit again.

He had known he wouldn't. Not in this life anyway.

# Strangers in Distress

*Do not forget to entertain strangers, for by so doing some people have entertained angels without knowing it.*

HEBREWS 13:2

*M*ichelle Bove is a warm, gracious person, but she has always been timid. She, her husband, and three young children live in a pleasant section of Manhattan Beach in Brooklyn, New York, about a block from the shore, an area where few needy people congregate.

One winter night as Michelle drove home from a meeting, she began praying that she could overcome her fearfulness. But she didn't expect her plea to be answered quite so soon! As she reached home and began to pull into her driveway, she saw two people standing in the middle of the street. Michelle was apprehensive, since the strangers were blocking her way, but she got out and asked them what they wanted.

The man, older and well dressed, certainly didn't look like a street person. Yet he asked Michelle to help his companion, a woman in her thirties.

"What do you need?" Michelle asked the woman.

"A place to sleep," the woman responded quietly. She was dressed shabbily but seemed to be intelligent. And she had the most beautiful blue eyes Michelle had ever seen.

Michelle hesitated, then turned back to the man. But he was no longer there! Michelle hadn't heard him say good-bye or step away, and although she looked up and down the quiet street, there was no sign of anyone there.

Michelle's first response to this extremely peculiar situation was a desire to flee to the safety of her home. But an inner urge stopped her. She had prayed for bravery, hadn't she? Instead, she heard herself saying to the blue-eyed woman, "Why don't you come home with me?" The woman accepted the invitation.

First Michelle phoned local motels, but no rooms were available. She then called a few nearby churches, but none could or would help. Michelle was becoming nervous. Her husband, who had been asleep when she arrived home, had awakened and demanded that she send the woman away. "He thinks I'm an easy mark, far too trusting," Michelle explains. Her husband was also concerned that Michelle had brought a stranger into their home, perhaps putting their children at risk, and he wanted her to *do something about it now*. Aggravated, he went back to bed, assuming Michelle would carry out his wishes.

Since the house is quite large, Michelle instead brought the woman to the basement-level guest room, fixed her some food, and made up a bed for her. The visitor had been almost completely silent up until now, but Michelle's disagreement with her husband triggered a response. "I've had problems with my husband too," she told Michelle.

"Do you have children?" Michelle asked.

"Yes, two."

"Then why are you alone? How did you get into this situation?"

Michelle's guest was evasive. It appeared she was in distress, running from something, and Michelle's concern increased. What had she gotten herself into? But she couldn't bring herself to ask a person in such a precarious position to leave, not in the middle of a cold night.

Instead, while the woman slept, Michelle sat upstairs in her kitchen, worrying. What if the woman intended to harm Michelle's family? What if the man who disappeared was this woman's accomplice, and he returned to rob them? And what would her husband say when he discovered that Michelle had let a stranger sleep in their home all night? Michelle prayed, read the Bible, and kept watch.

As dawn was breaking, Michelle packed some food and warm clothes and wrote down the names of shelters she had been unable to reach earlier. Then she awakened the woman. "You'll have to leave before my husband gets up," she told her. "I can't drive you anywhere because my children will be needing me soon."

"What is your name?" the woman asked. Michelle told her, putting the package into her arms.

"Thank you, Michelle," the woman said, and smiled. She looked much healthier, and her blue eyes shone. "I will never forget your kindness."

"Take care." Michelle opened the back door, closed it behind the visitor, and stood by the window to watch her walk down the driveway, which was the only way the woman could get out of Michelle's enclosed yard and onto the street. Not until the woman passed her, would Michelle feel truly safe.

Michelle waited...and waited...but the stranger never appeared. Like the man who had accompanied her, the woman had simply vanished.

Michelle will never be sure why the man or the young

woman stood in front of *her* house and asked *her* to respond despite her fear. But she has never been quite so timid since that day.

And while we're thinking about Michelle, we might consider a similar story, but with the opposite resolution.

Michigan resident Helen Griffith and members of her church group were winding down for the day the children's summer Bible-school program. Eight or nine women and some youngsters were standing by the room's entrance. "We were all caught up in our activities, collecting money, picking up materials, laughing, eating, busy-busy-busy ... " Helen recalls.

Suddenly a pale young woman came into the building and hesitantly approached the group standing near the door. "Excuse me," the woman said, speaking barely above a whisper. She looked exhausted. "Could I borrow some money from you ladies? To buy gas?" She had to get to a town about seventy miles away, she explained. Her frailness was evident, and Helen noticed she was expecting a baby.

Someone in the group quickly got the young woman a chair. Then everyone moved away to converse among themselves. Helen had only some change with her, but she suggested that they donate something from the school fund or take up a collection among themselves.

But one of the women objected. "We shouldn't help these kind of people, Helen," she said firmly. "They go from church to church playing on people's sympathies. Well, this one isn't getting anything from me!"

Several of the others nodded slowly, allowing themselves to be persuaded. "Why don't we send her to one of the other churches instead?" one suggested. "There's a church pantry not too far from here—they might help."

The young woman's face fell when a spokesperson went to her with a negative reply. She got up and walked heavily out the side door. Immediately Helen's conscience began to bother her, so she followed the woman outside, thinking she would give her what she had in her purse.

"But there was no one there," Helen relates. "No car, no young woman...I was only a few steps behind her, and she certainly wasn't walking quickly, but I saw no car moving through any of the lots or drives. She had disappeared."

To this day, Helen wonders if her church group was visited by an angel and had failed the test of kindness. "She came, asked quietly for assistance—and we who were so busy *talking* about love and kindness failed to *act* on our principles," she says. "We were hypocrites, and how I wish we had a chance to undo the mistake we made."

Why would an angel in human form appear in distress? Surely celestial beings have no angry husbands, no children, no worries at all! Maybe they become vulnerable for our sake, to offer us a chance to reach out, to trust, and to grow in the giving.

# Angels with Nightsticks

*For he will command his angels concerning you to guard you in all your ways...*

PSALMS 91:11

Steven Rogers was a rookie officer in the Nutley, New Jersey, police department in 1977 when he was assigned to be partners with Phil. Not only was Phil older and wiser, he was also an outspoken Christian. For the impulsive and sometimes rebellious Steve, Phil became a role model. Daily, before their shift, the two men would pray or read from the Bible, often reciting the Ninety-first Psalm, the one that commits us to God's care and summons angels when we are in danger.

Nutley had a growing problem. Recreational areas were being overrun with teenagers drinking, taking drugs, and vandalizing property. Police knew where the kids congregated, but whenever they raided the gatherings, most slipped away and could not be found. Apparently the teens had a hideout—but where? None of the police officers had been able to find it.

One day Steve and Phil were assigned to plainclothes duty. They were to dress like the kids and, it was hoped, discover their hideout and the source of their drugs. That night they stationed themselves in a secluded wooded area and watched the young people fighting, cursing, and destroying property.

"What I saw sickened me," Steve relates. "I realized we were not dealing with a few kids 'having fun,' but with many who were hard-core drug addicts with minds out of control. Many were invoking Charles Manson, or performing obscene acts. If this behavior spread, it could threaten the whole city."

The main source of the drugs, it appeared, was a young man the officers dubbed Mr. Big because of his apparent emotional hold on the group.

The next day the officers went to the scene of the gathering, prayed for guidance, and began to check it inch by inch. They soon came across a well-worn path covered with branches. The path led to a cleverly concealed cave. Inside, the officers found pills, liquor, pornographic material, and marijuana. Here was where so many young people eluded the police. That night, they decided, they would raid the cave.

Before their shift, they requested extra backup, but they were told they were on their own. How could two officers handle a bunch of aggressive kids all alone? Once again, the men prayed the Ninety-first Psalm. Then they strolled toward the crowd already gathering near a railroad embankment. Mr. Big was there, they noted. "We wanted to apprehend him first, because we felt many of the kids would discontinue their illegal activities if he wasn't around," Steve explains.

But as they approached, a girl recognized them. "Cops!" she screamed. The crowd scattered. Steve and Phil went after the girl, caught her, and called for a backup squad. By now some of the others, they knew, would be hidden in the cave.

Despite the fact that they were hopelessly outnumbered,

they found the hidden path and walked boldly into the entrance. "Freeze!" Steve shouted, and not a person in the cave moved. Steve ran his eyes across the group. At least twelve of them. And they had caught Mr. Big!

Phil walked over to Mr. Big and asked for the package he was holding. Meekly the young man handed over a bag of pills. Steve gathered other evidence, read everyone his rights, then stood in bewilderment, staring at the cave floor covered with submissive teens who could have easily overpowered the two officers. Why hadn't they put up a fight?

The van pulled up, and as they led the prisoners out of the cave, Steve turned to Mr. Big. "Why didn't you or any of the others try to attack us when we came in?"

"You think I'm crazy or something?" Mr. Big asked. "There were at least twenty guys in blue uniforms, and it would have been stupid to think of fighting or running."

"Twenty? No, there were just the two of us."

"Yeah?" Mr. Big called to another young prisoner. "Belinda, how many cops came into the cave?"

Belinda shrugged. "At least twenty-five."

It was then that Steve remembered the words he and Phil recited so faithfully: "You will not fear the terror of the night ...for he will command his angels concerning you...."

Within nine months of the time Steve and Phil had been assigned to this special duty, they had made 250 arrests— more than the department's annual total. Former hangouts of drug addicts and vandals were deserted, and Nutley neighborhoods flourished. Whenever anyone complimented the officers on their accomplishments, they gave credit to Jesus for protecting them and helping them solve the crimes.

Jesus...and a very special squad in blue.[22]

# Heavenly Housekeeper

*A ministering angel shall my sister be.*
SHAKESPEARE, *HAMLET*

$\mathcal{R}$aymond Herzing's mother, Mag, a Bavarian immigrant, settled in Lancaster, Pennsylvania, married, and had three children. The older two died in their twenties. Raymond, the youngest, became a priest in 1938. When Raymond's father died, his mother was alone, with no grandchildren or extended family nearby to take care of her. Since Raymond was now secretary to the bishop of Buffalo, New York, he found it harder and harder to look after his aging mother. He traveled regularly from his Buffalo residence to Lancaster, but couldn't keep up with everything Mag needed. And when he wasn't with his mother, he was worrying about her.

Raymond decided to employ a woman to live with Mag. Unfortunately, Mag was growing crotchety, and none of the women her son hired remained with her for long—with the whims of old age, Mag would constantly dismiss them. "This one didn't cook right, that one doesn't keep house the way she should...none of them are working out!" a frustrated Raymond once told a relative. He was spending more and more time with his mother, and neglecting his growing responsibilities in Buffalo.

Finally Raymond prayed. "God, if you want me to work

for You in Buffalo, You've got to help me with my mother here!"

Some time later Raymond was at his mother's home when a middle-aged woman knocked on the front door. She was neatly dressed and wore a pleasant expression. "I hear you are looking for someone to take care of your mother," she said.

"You heard right," Raymond told her, opening the door wider. "Won't you come in and talk about it?" He liked the woman instantly. She had a tranquil, kind air about her.

"I'd be willing to stay a year or so," she told him.

A year! Raymond couldn't believe God's benevolence. "That would be wonderful, providing my mother likes you," Raymond explained. "She can be, er ... rather difficult."

The woman just smiled.

Briskly Raymond outlined her duties and her salary. "What is your name?" he asked. "How should I make out your checks?"

"Oh...." The woman laughed a little. "Just call me Angel. And as far as my salary ... why don't we see how your mother feels about me first?"

Yes, that would be the challenge, Raymond agreed. If Angel wanted to test the waters, he certainly didn't blame her. He returned to Buffalo, cautiously optimistic.

Angel proved to be beyond worth. Mag accepted her right away, and the two got along famously. Raymond assumed someone in the neighborhood had sent Angel, but as time passed, he learned that none of the neighbors had ever met her before she came to live with Mag. Angel also seemed reticent about her background, never discussing how she happened to knock on his mother's door. Perhaps he should have asked for references. But Mag liked her so very much.

From time to time, Raymond brought up the subject of Angel's salary, but she always interrupted his concerns and waved them away. "I can't use the money now," she'd say. "We'll settle up when your mother no longer needs me." It seemed almost too good to be true, but by this time, Raymond was director of the Buffalo Family Life Office and steeped in additional duties. As long as his mother was safe and happy, he wasn't about to pressure Angel about anything!

About a year after Angel came, Mag Herzing died. "I don't think I'll go to the funeral," Angel told Raymond that morning. "I'll straighten up here instead." Raymond agreed. But when he returned to his mother's house after the burial, it seemed strangely empty.

"Angel?" he called, looking through the neat but deserted rooms. "Are you here?" But Angel was nowhere to be found, and her possessions were gone. Nor had Raymond ever paid her! And she had lived there, just as she'd predicted, for a year....

Angel went as mysteriously as she had come. But until his death in 1965, Monsignor Raymond Herzing always regarded her as a special answer to prayer.

# Leonor's Choice

*Gabriel blew, and a clean thin sound of perfect pitch*
*and crystalline delicacy filled all the universe to the*
*farthest star... as thin as the line separating past*
*from future...*

ISAAC ASIMOV, *"THE LAST TRUMP"*

Perhaps a book like this would not be complete without including a near-death experience where the person actually met her angel.

At eighteen, Leonor Reyes married David, who was only a year older. David received his draft notice a month after the wedding and had already reached Vietnam when Leonor began having health problems. She had developed a goiter in her neck that appeared to be malignant.

In February 1969, David's fifth month in Vietnam, his young bride underwent surgery to remove the growth. But during the operation it seemed the anesthesia was wearing off. "Suddenly I began rising, as if sitting up," Leonor wrote. "I could see the part of the operating room toward my feet; I could see my body lying on the table with my neck still open, and my head tilted way back.... Then I entered a place where there was total light. Others seemed to be around me, and someone at my left said, 'Do not look around or turn back.'"

Leonor obeyed. Gradually she realized that the beings

around her were angels. "You are going to meet someone who is very special to you," the being on her left told her. "Do not be anxious. You will be very happy. He is expecting you." Leonor looked down and saw what looked like white clouds, although she couldn't see her feet.

*Could I be on my way to see God?* she wondered. She felt ashamed at her own unworthiness, yet excited too. She grew more and more exultant as her journey continued.

Leonor and her celestial companions halted on the bank of a beautiful river with a green meadow beyond it. The angels began to rejoice, and Leonor saw a figure in white coming from among the trees in the distance. It was Jesus! She wanted to run toward him, but the river was dividing them. Jesus walked across the surface of the water toward her, and she was filled with love and wonder.

"I know you have been tired, sick, and worried," he said in the gentlest voice she had ever heard. "Would you like to come and be with me now?"

"Oh, yes!" She reached for his hand, then stopped. "But ... what about my husband? My mother? If I died now, it would hurt them so much. My husband might even get wounded when he hears the news." Leonor wanted nothing more than to stay with Jesus forever, but something held her back.

The man in white seemed pleased by her concern. "You can see your husband now if you wish," he told her. "Then you have a choice to make. You can come with me, or *both* of you can come. Or, if you wish, neither of you will come at this time. It will be up to you."

How could Leonor see David? Wasn't Vietnam half a world away? But she remembered that God could do everything, so she turned away. Two angels traveled with her a very long distance through an atmosphere of pure light.

"And there we were, standing behind a tree. One of the angels looked out. 'You see?' he said to me. 'There he is.'"

Leonor looked around the tree, as the angel had done, and saw David lying on his stomach in a bunker on top of a hill next to a fellow soldier. They were engaged in combat with the Viet Cong.

"Remember," the other angel told her, "you must choose."

Leonor thought of how wonderful it would be for her and David to leave this difficult world behind and be with God forever. But she also thought of both their mothers. If Leonor's death would be hard for them to bear, what of a double loss? Perhaps their parents would even doubt God's goodness if both of their youngsters were taken. Leonor didn't want that to happen.

"Quickly!" the angels told her.

"No!" Leonor cried. "No—we cannot hurt our parents this way!" At that very moment she saw a hand, almost invisible, reach down and cup over a grenade that had landed right next to David. David was safe.

Now Leonor in the company of many angels began hurrying on a journey through bright light. She began to grow weary, and beings on each side supported her. "We must hurry if you still want to return," they told her. At that moment, Leonor felt energy running through her body.

"Leonor, wake up, wake up...." Someone was calling her name.

"I'm here," she said. "I'm here." She saw two nurses bending over her, talking to each other, but she could not hear what they were saying. "I'm here," she said louder, and both looked at her in surprise.

"We were about to give up on you," one said softly.

Leonor's growth had indeed been malignant. But the doctor performed a total thyroidectomy, and although Leonor has had some health problems since her surgery, no signs of cancer have ever recurred.

Even more important to this young bride, her husband returned safe and sound from Vietnam. Years later, Leonor asked him if he was ever in a bunker on a hill with another soldier when a grenade fell next to him during combat.

"Only once," David answered. "But the grenade was a dud. Boy, was I glad!"

# The Day We Saw the Angels

> [Patriarch Tychon] was seized with a kind of ecstacy
> and overheard the singing of angels, the beauty of
> which he was afterwards unable to describe; neither
> could he at the moment grasp the words of that song,
> but was aware of it only as the harmony of many
> voices.
>
> A TREASURY OF RUSSIAN SPIRITUALITY

$\mathscr{P}$erhaps there would be no better way to conclude these stories than with one from Dr. S. Ralph Harlow, who first shared it with readers of *Guideposts* magazine*:

It was not Christmas, it was not even wintertime, when the event occurred that for me threw sudden new light on the ancient angel tale. It was a glorious spring morning and we were walking, my wife and I, through the newly budded birches and maples near Ballardvale, Massachusetts.

Now I realize that this, like any account of personal experience, is only as valid as the good sense and honesty of the person relating it. What can I say about myself? That I am a scholar who shuns guesswork and admires scientific investigation? That I have an A.B. from Harvard, an M.A.

---

from Columbia, a PhD from Hartford Theological Seminary? That I have never been subject to hallucinations? That attorneys have solicited my testimony and I have testified in the courts, regarded by judge and jury as a faithful reliable witness? All this is true, and yet I doubt any amount of credentials can influence the belief or disbelief of another.

In the long run, each of us must sift what comes to us from others through his own life experience, his view of the universe. And so I will simply tell my story.

The little path on which Marion and I walked that May morning was spongy to our steps, and we held hands with the sheer delight of life as we strolled near a lovely brook. It was May, and because it was the examination reading period at Smith College where I was a professor, we were able to get away for a few days to visit Marion's parents.

We frequently took walks in the country, and we especially loved the spring after a hard New England winter, for it is then that the fields and the woods are radiant and calm yet show new life bursting from the earth. This day we were especially happy and peaceful; we chatted sporadically, with great gaps of satisfying silence between our sentences.

Then from behind us we heard the murmur of muted voices in the distance, and I said to Marion, "We have company in the woods this morning."

Marion nodded, and turned to look. We saw nothing, but the voices were coming nearer—at a faster pace than we were walking—and we knew that the strangers would soon overtake us. Then we perceived that the sounds were not only behind us but above us, and we looked up.

How can I describe what we felt? Is it possible to tell of the surge of exaltation that ran through us? Is it possible to record this phenomenon in objective accuracy and yet be credible?

For about ten feet above us and slightly to our left was a floating group of glorious beautiful creatures that glowed with spiritual beauty. We stopped and stared as they passed above us.

There were six of them, young beautiful women dressed in flowing white garments and engaged in earnest conversation. If they were aware of our existence they gave no indication of it. Their faces were perfectly clear to us, and one woman, slightly older than the rest, was especially beautiful. Her dark hair was pulled back in what today we would call a ponytail and although I cannot say it was bound at the back of her head, it appeared to be. She was talking intently to a younger spirit whose back was toward us and who looked up into the face of the woman who was talking.

Neither Marion nor I could understand their words although their voices were clearly heard. The sound was somewhat like hearing but being unable to understand a group of people talking outside a house with all the windows and doors shut.

They seemed to float past us and their graceful motion seemed natural—as gentle and peaceful as the morning itself. As they passed, their conversation grew fainter and fainter until it faded out entirely, and we stood transfixed on the spot, still holding hands and still with the vision before our eyes. It would be an understatement to say we were astounded. Then we looked at each other, each wondering if the other also had seen.

There was a fallen birch tree just there beside the path. We sat down on it and I said, "Marion, what did you see?

Tell me exactly, in precise detail. And tell me what you heard."

She knew my intent—to test my own eyes and ears to see if I had been the victim of hallucination or imagination. And her reply was identical in every way to what my own senses had reported to me.

I have related this story with the same faithfulness and respect for truth and accuracy as I would tell it on the witness stand. But even as I record it, I know how incredible it sounds.

Perhaps I can claim no more for it than that it has had a deep effect on our own lives.... Since Marion and I began to be aware of the host of heaven all about us, our lives have been filled with a wonderful hope. Phillips Brooks, the great Episcopal bishop, expressed the cause of this hope more beautifully than I can do:

"This is what you are to hold fast to yourself—the *sympathy and companionship of the unseen worlds*. No doubt it is best for us now that they should be unseen. It cultivates that higher perception that we call 'faith.' But who can say that the time will not come when, even to those who live here upon earth, the unseen worlds shall no longer be unseen?"

The experience at Ballardvale, added to the convictions of my Christian faith, gives me not only a feeling of assurance about the future, but a sense of adventure toward it too.

# Another Beginning

*I will not wish thee riches nor the glow of greatness,*
  *but that wherever thou go*
  *some weary heart shall gladden at thy smile,*
  *or shadowed life know sunshine for a while.*
*And so thy path shall be a track of light,*
  *like angels' footsteps passing through the night.*

WORDS ON A CHURCH WALL IN UPWALTHAM, ENGLAND

*P*eople in our culture are uncomfortable with the notion of angels in today's world. When we can explain something, we call it a "natural occurrence." But when we cannot explain it, we shrink from labeling it "supernatural." Yet how many of us, in moments when life has seemed most frightening or painful or bewildering, have heard a whisper, felt an invisible hand on our shoulder, been helped by a stranger who was just like us...and yet, somehow, *not* like us? At times when we have felt abandoned and alone, how many of us have been touched by a mysterious, unexplainable encounter that has given us the courage and the strength we needed to go on?

Why is it necessary to explain such occurrences? Why *wouldn't* a loving God, intimately concerned with His children, send angels *and* humans to do His work?

For what is it that angels do? They bring us good news.

They open our eyes to moments of wonder, to lovely possibilities, to exemplary people, to the idea that God is here in our midst. They lift our hearts and give us wings.

We can do that for each other.

Angels minister to us. They sit silently with us as we mourn. They offer us opportunities to turn our suffering into bridges of healing and hope. They challenge us toward new understanding, fresh perspective.

We can do that for each other.

Angels offer practical help. As we've seen, they furnish information, provide food, buffer the storms of life. Angels lead everyone in the same direction, although not everyone travels at the same speed. But angels are willing to stand by—and wait.

We can do that for each other.

"There is one trouble with full-time angels; they are completely unpredictable and you cannot send out for one," Lee Ballard, the man who met Pug-Pug, reminds us. "That is why part-time angels are so important. Part-time angels like you and me."

Few of us may identify a celestial being during our lifetime (although I am sure each of us has been touched by them). But we can all be angels to one another. We can choose to obey the still small stirring within, the little whisper that says, "Go. Ask. Reach out. Be an answer to someone's plea. You have a part to play. Have faith." We can decide to risk that He is indeed there, watching, caring, cherishing us as we love and accept love.

The world will be a better place for it.

And wherever they are, the angels will dance.

# Notes

1. F. S. Smythe, *Camp Six*, An Account of the 1933 Mount Everest Expedition (London: Hodder and Stroughton, Ltd., 1937), p. 262.
2. Raymond Woolsey, *Joy in the Morning* (Washington, D.C.: Review and Herald Publishing, 1978), p. 182.
3. Charles and Frances Hunter, *Angels on Assignment* (Kingwood, TX: Hunter Books, 1979), p. 183.
4. Corrie ten Boom, *A Prisoner and Yet...* (Toronto, Canada: Evangelical Publishers, 1947), p. 10.
5. Corrie ten Boom, *The Hiding Place* (New York: Bantam Books, 1981), pp. 202-203.
6. Gordon Lindsay, *Ministry of Angels* (Dallas: Christ for the Nations, 1974), p. 26.
7. Dawn Adrian Adams, Ph.D., "Rain," *Guideposts*, July 1991, p. 38.
8. Betty Malz, *Angels Watching Over Me* (Old Tappen, NJ: Chosen Books, 1986). Reprinted with permission.
9. Lee Ballard, "The Flutter of Wings," *Dallas* magazine, May 1986. Condensed and reprinted with permission.
10. W. Doyle Gulligan, ed., *Devotion to the Holy Angels* (Houston: Lumen Christi Press, 1990), p. 101.
11. Malcolm Muggeridge, *Something Beautiful for God* (New York: Ballantine Books, 1971), p. 41.
12. From "I Too Saw an Angel" by Raymond Edman, originally published in *Bulletin of Wheaton College*, December 1959. Retold with permission.
13. Hope Price, "He Will Send Angels," *Fate*, May 1961. Reprinted with permission.
14. Billy Graham, *Angels: God's Secret Agents* (New York: Doubleday, 1975), pp. 2-3.
15. Gulligan, *Devotion*, p. 98.
16. Corrie ten Boom, *Marching Orders for the End Battle* (Fort Washington, PA: Christian Literature Crusade, 1969), pp. 89-90.
17. Graham, *Angels*, p. 3.
18. W. A. Spicer, *Stories of Providential Deliverance* (Washington: Review & Herald Publishing, 1936), p. 33.
19. Basilea Schlink, *The Unseen World of Angels and Demons* (Old Tappan, NJ: Chosen Books, 1986), p. 137.

20. Taken from anecdotes and from *Send Me Your Guardian Angel* by Alessio Parente (Amsterdam, NY: Noteworthy Co., 1983). For more information on Padre Pio, contact the National Centre for Padre Pio, 11 North Whitehall Road, Norristown, PA, 19403.
21. Retold with the permission of Pastor LaVerne Tucker, Director, The Quiet Hour, a worldwide mission outreach headquartered in Redlands, CA.
22. Sergeant Steven Rogers heads 777th Precinct (P. O. Box 72, Dayton, NJ 08810), an organization for police officers and their families. He has written a book and appears twice weekly on "Police Desk," the only radio program in America hosted by a police officer.

## Bibliography and Additional Reading

Adler, Mortimer J. *The Angels and Us*. New York: Macmillan, 1982.

Angelica, Mother Mary. *Sons of Light*. Birmingham, AL: Our Lady of Angels Monastery, 1976.

Burnham, Sophy. *A Book of Angels*. New York: Ballantine Books, 1990.

Gilmore, Don G. *Angels, Angels Everywhere*. New York: Paragon House, 1988.

Godwin, Malcolm. *Angels, an Endangered Species*. New York: Simon & Schuster, 1990.

Graham, Billy. *Angels: God's Secret Agents*. New York: Doubleday, 1975.

Gulligan, W. Doyle, ed. *Devotion to the Holy Angels*. Houston: Lumen Christi Press, 1990.

Hunter, Charles and Frances. *Angels on Assignment*. Kingwood, TX: Hunter Books, 1979.

Lindsay, Gordon. *Ministry of Angels*. Dallas: Christ for the Nations, 1974.

MacDonald, Hope. *When Angels Appear*. Grand Rapids, MI: Zondervan, 1982.

MacGreggor, Geddes. *Angels, Ministers of Grace*. New York: Paragon House, 1988.

Malz, Betty. *Angels Watching Over Me*. New York: Chosen Books, 1986.

# Bibliography and Additional Reading

Muggeridge, Malcolm. *Something Beautiful for God*. New York: Ballantine Books, 1971.

Parente, Alessio. *Send Me Your Guardian Angel*. Amsterdam, NY: Noteworthy, 1983.

Paretti, Frank. *This Present Darkness*. Westchester, IL: Crossway Books, 1986.

———. *Piercing the Darkness*. Westchester, IL: Crossway Books, 1990.

Ronner, John. *Do You Have a Guardian Angel?*. Indialantic, FL: Mamre Press, 1985.

Schlink, Basilea. *The Unseen World of Angels and Demons*. Old Tappan, NJ: Chosen Books, 1986.

ten Boom, Corrie. *A Prisoner and Yet....* Toronto, Canada: Evangelical Publishers, 1947.

———. *Marching Orders for the End Battle*. Fort Washington, PA: Christian Literature Crusade, 1969.

———. *The Hiding Place*. New York: Bantam Books, 1981.

Woolsey, Raymond. *Joy in the Morning*. Washington: Review and Herald Publishing, 1978.

## Some Angel Resources

Angel Collectors Club of America, 533 E. Fairmont Drive, Tempe, AZ 85282.

Marilynn's Angels (a business dealing in angel products), 275 Celeste, Riverside, CA 92507.

Mamre Press (catalog has some angel books), 107 Second Avenue, Murfreesboro, TN 37130

Opus Sanctorum Angelorum (Work of the Holy Angels), a worldwide Catholic organization that is devoted to explaining and encouraging devotion to angels: P. O. Box 15314, Philadelphia, PA 19111.

## Author's Afterword

I am always interested in hearing from people who believe that they have had an angel experience. If you would like to share your experience, please write to me at P. O. Box 1694, Arlington Heights, IL 60006.

—*J. W. A.*